LIBRARY GUIDING

a program for exploiting
library resources

LIBRARY GUIDING

a program for exploiting library resources

R J P CAREY

BA DipNZLS FLA

CLIVE BINGLEY **b** LONDON

FIRST PUBLISHED 1974 BY CLIVE BINGLEY LTD
16 PEMBRIDGE ROAD LONDON W11
SET IN 10 ON 13 POINT LINOTYPE BASKERVILLE
AND PRINTED IN THE UK BY THE CENTRAL PRESS (ABERDEEN) LTD
COPYRIGHT © R J P CAREY 1974
ALL RIGHTS RESERVED
0 85157 167 0

Contents

Illustrations

8 *a* Receiving instruction in catalogue use at Hofstra University, New York, USA.

b Kodak Miracode microfilm reader with printout facility.

Foreword

THIS MANUAL HAS BEEN written as the result of a number of years of work in giving library instruction to groups of students at a college of technology; and of the findings of a survey on the methods of teaching; and also of the subject content of library instruction in the colleges and universities of Britain, in the USA, and in some other overseas countries.

During this survey, correspondence took place with some 350 college and university librarians, eighty of whom were visited. From these visits it was found that, even for a librarian, most libraries were difficult to use; that is, it was difficult to find out what facilities the library had to offer, where the books and services were located, and how, for instance, one should use the catalogue.

As far as the students were concerned, the major effort to overcome these difficulties took some form of personal library instruction. Such library instruction suffers from a number of weaknesses. Many librarians reported a shortage of time, of funds, and of qualified library staff, with a consequent difficulty in operating library courses. Students often felt that library instruction was not necessary to their studies, and that, if it were necessary, it did not come at a time when they really needed it. Teachers frequently considered that time given by students to library instruction could be more profitably spent studying for examination subjects.

The notes in this manual seek to show a way of overcoming some of these difficulties, by a systems approach to library guiding and the use of audio visual aids for instruction within the library.

The most important purpose of this manual is to save wasted time for library users and for librarians, and at the same time to provide, on a self-service basis, wider experience in handling information for all kinds of library user.

Individual libraries have widely differing needs and some of the most useful information about exploitation techniques will come from an examination of systems and aids used in working libraries. For this reason, included in the text are several examples of scripts for pre-recorded instruction and illustrations of audio visual aids and equipment. The inclusion of this material has been possible because of the co-operation of librarians and others who have given their time and advice so generously. This help has been very greatly appreciated.

Acknowledgements

FOR PERMISSION TO USE scripts, photographs and other information, I wish to express my thanks to: W Scobbie, County Librarian, Lanarkshire, Scotland; A White, Western Australian Institute of Technology, Bentley, WA; W Wright, Royal Aircraft Establishment, England; C W J Wilson, Atomic Energy Research Establishment, England; M N Paton, County Librarian, Renfrew, Scotland; A Wallace, County Librarian, Newcastle-upon-Tyne, England; Mrs J Goring, West Norwood Library, Lambeth Public Libraries, London; J J Gardner and Mrs K Roos, Model Library Program, Massachusetts Institute of Technology, USA; O B Ramsay, Eastern Michigan University, USA; A R Samuels, Hofstra University, USA; Miss A Olivier-Wright, Central Office of Information, London; J Parfitt, Dacorum College, Hemel Hempstead, England; A C Bubb and Miss A Lumb, University of Salford, England; Miss J Hardy, Imperial College, London; T H Cannon, Office for Scientific and Technical Information, London.

I also wish to thank my wife for reading my proofs and for her support and encouragement at all times. My thanks go, too, to my colleagues at Hatfield; to the teachers and librarians who helped to produce and test audio-visual materials; and, especially to the Leverhulme Research Awards Committee, whose generosity made possible the extension of my early experiments.

1

Introduction

PEOPLE USING A LIBRARY usually want the answer to three broad questions.

First of all, *what books and services can the library offer me, the reader?* For example, has the library important periodical collections; what titles are regularly received and what length of run is held; what published abstracts and periodical indexes are received; is there a collection of British Standards; what kind of careers information is available; are there any microtext readers; what photocopying facilities are offered; does the library lend tape recordings or gramophone records; what kind of equipment may be used or borrowed; is there a typewriter; can tape recorders be borrowed for home use?

These are just a few of the queries which relate to a modern library. There are many others. Once the reader is aware of the books and services which are available the next difficulty is *to find the facility which is needed.* The reader can, of course, ask a member of the library staff, but often the problem is not as simple as this and the larger the library the more complex the problem becomes. Very often a reader does not know precisely what he or she wants and the member of staff able to help may not be available; also, for effective use of any library, it is necessary to have some understanding of the pattern behind its organisation.

Finally, having found the required document or service, the library user very frequently wants to know *how to use what he has found effectively*; and, with a minimum of wasted time. What, for instance, are the principles behind the classification scheme which the library uses; what kind of documents are recorded in the catalogue; does the catalogue record only the items in the user's own library; does the catalogue include books and other documents kept by other libraries; what are the various parts of the catalogue; what is the function of each part; what is the meaning of the symbols used on a catalogue entry; how does one find a book recorded in the catalogue? How does one operate the photocopying machine? How does one set about putting film on the microfilm reader; how can the image on the microfilm reader screen be sharpened? What are the abstracting publications; how does one set about tracing references; where can one find the full titles of periodicals which are recorded, in the abstract, in abbreviated form; what is the significance of numbers given in heavy type as part of the bibliographic detail?

Having considered the three queries, what can the library offer, where is it to be found and how can it be used, the next difficulty in making information in a library accessible is that each individual coming to the library uses it in a different way on different occasions. Today, a reader may want simply to check the spelling of a word in an English dictionary or to find the telephone number of a friend in Scotland. The same reader may on some other occasion wish to make a literature search on the subject of vitamin C deficiency in laboratory rats, or the drug problem in primary schools. Many students use the college library as a quiet place for private study or to do homework, making only occasional references to set books.

These differences in individual use depend upon two factors; the immediate requirements of the reader, and his previous experience in using information and libraries.

A guiding scheme designated to make libraries easy to use, that is, to make the information which the library contains more simply accessible to the users of it, seeks to answer the three queries what, where and how, in a way which will be suitable for each individual reader at the level appropriate to his or her previous library experience. The scheme is also designed to make readers more aware of the range and variety of information sources, so that they will make a wider and more effective use of information, therefore the guiding system has a direct teaching function. Although the author's experience has been mainly in college libraries, the scheme described in this manual can have equal application in a public, university, or special library. Such a system has the following elements:

1 *Permanent visual information*: Wall panels, hanging and standing signs, shelf labels.

2 *Information stations*: Pre-recorded information on tape, with printed explanatory charts or slides, which is available at relevant positions in the library. This information can be used by readers at any time without assistance from library staff.

3 *Printed guides*: These guides co-ordinate the various parts of the scheme and extend and amplify the information given on the wall panels and hanging signs. They also supplement the information supplied on the pre-recorded tapes.

4 *Coloured guiding signals*: For the purpose of this system the library is regarded as a number of geographical areas. Each area is allotted a colour and all documents and services within that area are identified by that colour. The chief purpose of these signals is to give mobility to the guiding system.

5 *Administrative routines*: These are necessary in order to keep information in any large academic library, supplied by the system, complete and up-to-date. For example, a *Guide to periodicals* requires monthly supplements to keep the information in it up to date.

In the following chapters various aspects of these elements will be discussed. General principles will be outlined and sample scripts for instructional tapes are analysed with suggestions for modification to suit the needs of individual libraries.

Several types of colour guiding schemes are illustrated; and, examples of some other guiding techniques used in the libraries of Britain and America are reviewed. Because of the difficulty in obtaining suitable hardware for a guiding program of this kind there are some notes on the practical problems involved, including brief construction details for setting up an inductive loop and some suggestions for assembling labels and wall panels.

Finally, we will consider how personal instruction and advice to readers fits into a guiding program; how exploitation, in the widest sense, has been influenced by the recent technological developments in microforms and in the machine retrieval of information; and, how librarians have attempted to evaluate the effect of exploitation techniques.

A systems approach to library guiding using coloured signals is, it is believed, a new concept in library technique. The system has already proved useful in libraries of various kinds. It is the purpose of this manual not only to discuss some of the existing schemes but to provide practical information which would enable any librarian to design and install a guiding system for his or her own library. The techniques and materials are simple and inexpensive, and, in a small library, a complete scheme can be designed and set up in a few hours.

2

Permanent visual information—
colour coded guiding

EVERY ORGANISATION WHICH OFFERS goods or services for sale
recognises the importance of making the customer aware of the
many opportunities he has for spending his money, taking care
to tell him how best he can take advantage of the good things
which are offered and where and how they may be purchased.
Part of this exploitation technique takes the form of advertising,
but a good deal of effort is also exerted within the place where
the customer comes in contact with the goods. At the airport the
arrivals and *departures* board sets out the number and time
of our flight and the places where the plane will stop on route.
Direction signs lead the passenger to the appropriate gate for the
required flight number. To reinforce this visual information, a
voice on the public address system keeps the passengers constantly
aware of the up-to-the-minute details of the flights, the times and
the possible delays or changes of plan.

Similarly, in the department store, wall panels record the
location and brief contents of each department; and, hanging
signs indicate where particular kinds of goods can be bought. In
travelling to different levels in the store a familiar voice informs
the customer of the joys which await him or her as each floor is
reached.

It is the business of a commercial trading concern to sell
products and services at a profit, and, in general, the larger the
amount sold, the greater the profit.

A library does not expect to make a monetary profit; but, in
its relationship with its readers or customers, it has many points
of similarity with a supermarket or a department store. It is
necessary to make its readers aware of the books and services
which are offered. It is helpful, too, if the reader can be told where

to find particular documents and services and very often he will want to know how to use what he has found. In such a program, the permanent visual information is the central part of the system. Although we are using the term *permanent* visual information, the detailed items of information will be expected to change as the library develops and grows.

Good guiding, in the form of clear easily read information, effective labels, and precise printed instructions, has long been recognised as an essential part of normal library management. However, a *system of guiding* as a means of leading readers to a wider, more understanding use of libraries, represents a new approach to the exploitation of library resources.

PRINCIPLES BEHIND SYSTEMS GUIDING

At this point it may be helpful to consider in rather more detail the elements of permanent visual information in a guiding system. The term 'guiding' in this context embraces all the aids and devices which a library employs to make its resources more easily accessible to its readers. In the first place, there are two principles behind such a system. The reader is not expected to rely on his or her memory, therefore much of the visual information is, necessarily, repeated in several places in the library. Secondly, the reader is led progressively from broad areas of information to specific details about the books and services which can be found in the library.

CHARACTERISTICS OF VISUAL INFORMATION

Such information can be seen by people coming to the library at any time. However, the reader, who may use the library for a different purpose each time he comes, only needs to use that part of the information which is relevant to the needs of the moment. Also such information should be simple enough to have meaning for the reader whatever his previous library experience.

WHERE SHOULD VISUAL INFORMATION BE SEEN?

The placing of contents panels or hanging signs and labels is a matter of common sense. Positioning will depend upon the needs and the facilities of each library and such information will be placed where library users will find it most useful.

A panel showing the broad organisation and *contents* of the library will be most helpful at or near the entrance to the library, preferably in a position where the panel can be seen even when the library is closed. As a means of making the library easier for readers to understand and use, this is the most important kind of information the library can offer. It may well be repeated at several points in the library especially where readers are likely to pause. For example, in a multi-storey library, stair landings provide a position which can be seen as the reader goes up or down the stairs, and where it is convenient to pause in order to read detailed information. In a larger library, each main area or department will call for a similar broad analysis of its content and organisation. This information will have most value for readers at the entrances to these departments; and once again, the information can be usefully repeated at various places in the department where readers are likely to pause or wait; for instance in a seated area for general reading, at the enquiry desk, or near the tables for private study. The readability of this general awareness information is an important factor. The actual height and breadth of the panels and the size of the lettering will depend upon the dimensions and proportions of each individual library; but it is suggested that a main contents panel should be readable, for one with normal eyesight, at a distance of at least twelve feet. When such information is repeated, say, in the reading area or at the inquiry desk, the size of the lettering can be proportionately reduced. *Specific* content or instruction panels or labels should, of course, be as near as possible to the relevant books and services. Instructions for using the catalogue will only be useful at the catalogue. Directions for using the photocopier should be on the machine itself. The list of subjects contained in a book stack will be most useful on the book stack end.

Further consideration will need to be given to visual information, which is designed to catch the eye from a distance so that required information may be selected from an array of signs which are at different distances from the observer. This factor is of

17

special importance when designing hanging signs, but we shall be discussing this subject more fully when we consider colour coded guiding.

In any detailed system of guiding it is important that the number of signs used should be the minimum necessary for effective guiding and the information on each panel, sign or label should be in the shortest form which will achieve its purpose. The language should be simple and direct with as few technical terms as possible. It is helpful for the library user if guidance and instruction is presented in a uniform sequence designed to answer the general questions, what is it, where is it, how should it be used?

Permanent visual information is of four broad kinds: *public relations* and library news; *content information; instruction* and memory jogging information; and lastly, *shelf labelling.*

Public relations information includes the usual notices about quietness and smoking, but the most effective device for keeping readers in touch with library activity is a well placed *library notice or news board* the purpose of which is to inform library users of library activity which is likely to affect them as readers; especially, of any changes and development in the library stock or services. Such information should be brief and changed frequently. The function of such a news board is also to draw attention to existing documents and services which, the librarian considers, could be more widely used by readers. When the reader's interest has been aroused by a brief announcement on the news board, more detailed information can be supplied by means of supplementary leaflets. It can be assumed that a reader who has become interested in a news item will be more likely to read the detailed information in a leaflet.

Contents information is designed to answer the general query, what has the library to offer. Such information may present a broad outline of the organisation of books and services or may be very specific. Figure 1 shows the contents panel of a small special library occupying three rooms and a cellar. Figure 2 indicates detailed specific information about the bibliographic

BOOKS AND PERIODICALS IN THIS LIBRARY

1   CIRCULATION AREA
    Issue desk, Current periodicals
    Catalogue, Pamphlets and
    information queries.

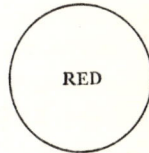

(RED)

2   REFERENCE ROOM
    Dictionaries, Encyclopedias,
    Directories, Law reports,
    Microfilm readers.

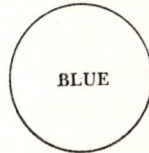

(BLUE)

3   MAIN READING ROOM
    Books for loan
    (UDC Subject order.)

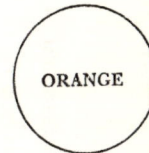

(ORANGE)

4   DOWN STAIRS (Key at desk)
    Back files of periodicals.

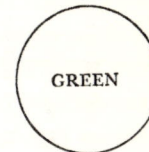

(GREEN)

Figure 1

INDEXING/ABSTRACTING PUBLICATIONS IN THIS LIBRARY

PHYSICS ABSTRACTS

ELECTRICAL AND ELECTRONIC ABSTRACTS

COMPUTER AND CONTROL ABSTRACTS

INSTRUMENT ABSTRACTS

ALUMINIUM ABSTRACTS

LEAD ABSTRACTS

METALLURGICAL ABSTRACTS

METALS ABSTRACTS

METAL FINISHING ABSTRACTS

CIRF ABSTRACTS

TECHNICAL EDUCATION ABSTRACTS

MANAGEMENT ABSTRACTS

BRITISH HUMANITIES INDEX

BRITISH EDUCATION INDEX

BUSINESS PERIODICALS INDEX

LIBRARY AND INFORMATION SCIENCE ABSTRACTS

AUTOMOBILE ABSTRACTS

Also:

GOVERNMENT PUBLICATIONS LISTS

(BRITAIN AND USA)

Note:

BRITISH TECHNOLOGY INDEX is filed with

ENCYCLOPEDIAS

Figure 2

aids shelved in a section of a college library. This label is placed next to the shelves holding the abstracts and periodicals indexes.

Instruction information is of many types and the language used and the amount of detail will depend upon the needs of the people using the library. All such instruction is concerned with simple principles which can be easily understood by most readers; and, frequently has a memory jogging function rather than a teaching one. In Figure 3, we see a book stack label for the abstracts section of a college library. The main purpose of the label is to inform the reader that in this set of shelves he will find *Analytical abstracts* and *Applied mechanics reviews* but there is

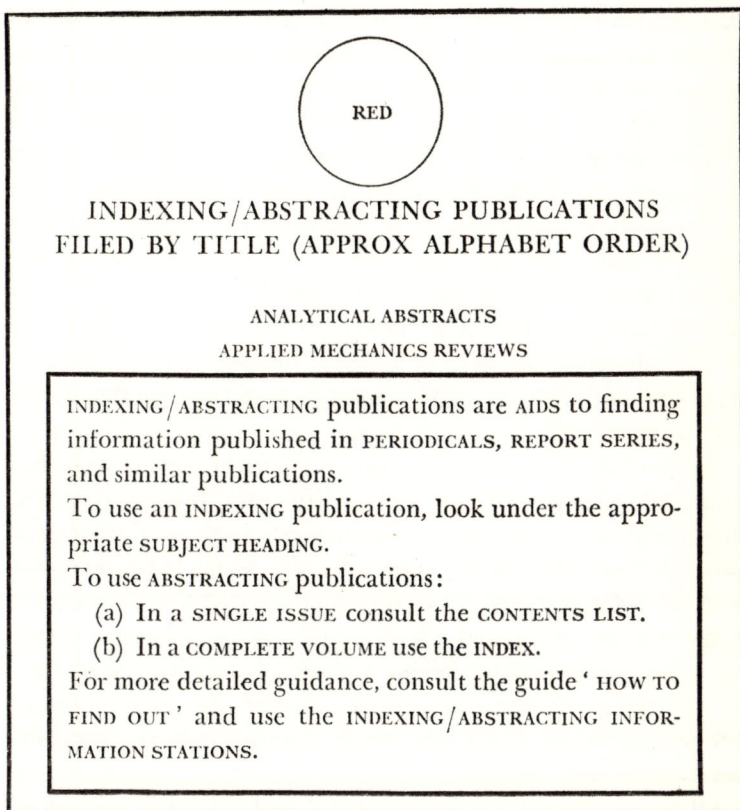

RED

INDEXING/ABSTRACTING PUBLICATIONS
FILED BY TITLE (APPROX ALPHABET ORDER)

ANALYTICAL ABSTRACTS
APPLIED MECHANICS REVIEWS

INDEXING/ABSTRACTING publications are AIDS to finding information published in PERIODICALS, REPORT SERIES, and similar publications.

To use an INDEXING publication, look under the appropriate SUBJECT HEADING.

To use ABSTRACTING publications:

    (a) In a SINGLE ISSUE consult the CONTENTS LIST.

    (b) In a COMPLETE VOLUME use the INDEX.

For more detailed guidance, consult the guide ' HOW TO FIND OUT ' and use the INDEXING/ABSTRACTING INFORMATION STATIONS.

Figure 3

also a reminder that the information in periodicals indexes and in abstracts is differently organised and that there are in the library two aids where he can obtain more detailed information about abstracts and indexes.

Shelf labelling is the visual information which can be most important in preventing waste of time for readers; especially, when seeking books of non-fiction and runs of periodicals. In a later chapter, we shall discuss some of the ways of producing shelf labels. However, as with other visual information, the reader needs a label which can be easily read at a distance. In practice it is frequently necessary to glance along a bay of shelves while standing in a narrow passage between book stacks. Readability depends on three factors, the light level in the area, the size of the lettering and the contrast between the lettering and the background of the label. A similar time saving function is provided by *guide cards* within a *card catalogue*. Easily read guide cards at intervals of about half an inch greatly speed up the use of a catalogue. In a classified catalogue, if these guide cards show the subject and the class number, readers using the catalogue quickly come to appreciate the significance of the principles behind the classification scheme. Finally, although the emphasis has been placed upon the time saving aspects of guiding for *readers,* it is perhaps more important in saving time for *library staff,* especially for junior and untrained staff amongst whom there is often a very fast turnover.

Colour coding and guiding. Colour coding of various kinds has been widely used in libraries for many years. Perhaps the most frequently used application of colour has been to denote categories of books for various uses, reference books which may not leave the library, books for short term loan, children's books, etc. A few libraries have used colour to indicate the subject content; one university librarian tried out a scheme using nineteen colours. A few public libraries have used coloured flashes to indicate different kinds of fiction (crime novels, adventure stories, historical novels, light romances, etc.).

All these applications are concerned with the classification of individual books. A red flash on a *reference* book informs the reader that the book can only be used in the library. If this information is not noticed or is ignored by the reader, on taking the book to the issue desk, the library assistant, seeing the red flash, is immediately alert to the fact that the book may not be issued. Where coloured signals have been used to denote, for example, the various classes of the Dewey Decimal Classification, such signals replace the class mark or are supplementary to it. This form of colour coding has had some success in a high school library, known to the writer, where the pupils know that if they want a book dealing with a science subject, there will be a blue circle on the spine and that the relevant book stack has over it a sign carrying a six inch circle of blue.

In a *system of guiding*, colour coding serves a somewhat different purpose. In a guiding scheme designed to lead the reader to the books he wants to use, *contents information* is not much help unless it is coupled with some means of directing him to the place in the library where the sought for documents or services are to be found. For this purpose, the library may be regarded as a series of geographical areas. Each area may then be allotted a colour and the documents and services within such an area can be identified by that colour. The first purpose of this application of colour coding is to give mobility to the guiding information. People who are familiar with the coloured direction lights in the stations of the London Underground Railway will know how simply this arrangement works.

Probably five or six different colours is a maximum which it is practicable to use. For the effective use of coloured signals it is necessary to have clear contrast between the colours. Also, five or six different colours is as large a number as can be remembered without effort. Such signals may use shape in addition to colour, when again, a clear contrast between shapes is important. In practice, circular, square and triangular signals will provide the necessary variety and detail of information. As will be seen from the examples of the guiding schemes in the working libraries which are described below, colours identify books and services which are listed on contents panels. The reader is led from the contents information to the required area by means of signals on overhead panels.

As a secondary purpose, colour coding can be used to denote groups or types of publication. This arrangement can be particularly suitable in a library which is divided into subject departments. In each department the same type of publication may be identified by the same colour. For example, *periodicals* may be coded blue, *bibliographic aids,* red, and the *catalogue,* yellow. A red signal will then identify the abstracts files in the science department, in the engineering department and in the humanities department. Similarly, a blue signal indicates where periodicals are filed in all departments of the library, while a yellow signal indicates where there is a catalogue whatever department the reader is using. This kind of colour coded guiding is completely flexible. It can be used for any kind of premises, any shape of building and any arrangement of books and services within the library. Also, it can identify any kind of document, any subject or any service.

As with all library fittings, the physical size of guiding elements is dependent upon the dimensions and proportions of the library premises. However, in the author's experience, a good working arrangement is to use overhead signs which are approximately eight feet from floor level. The signals then need to be six to seven inches in diameter and the lettering a little less than one inch high. The sign is approximately one foot deep. The length of these signs depends upon the number of signals required. Ten to twelve inches should be allowed for each signal. Materials, which can be used for making these signs, is discussed in some detail in a later chapter.

SOME GUIDING PATTERNS IN WORKING LIBRARIES

In each of the three examples which follow, the way in which each library is organised is different but there are three basic elements: *Content panels* at various levels of detail; overhead colour coded *direction signs;* and *instruction panels,* the most important of which provides guidance for using the catalogue. These instructions included: first, a brief statement of the principles behind the classification used by each particular library with specific examples relevant to the subjects of that library; secondly, a brief definition of the purpose of the catalogue and the range of documents recorded in it, followed by a description of the various parts of the catalogue with brief instructions for the use of each; lastly, an enlarged view of a catalogue card, with annotations explaining the various items of information on it. In the descriptions which follow, representative examples of these various aspects of the guiding scheme have been selected.

LIBRARY GUIDING PATTERN 1

This is a library of a technical college in West London which was located in a two storeyed three bedroom house, separate from the main college buildings. Except for the erection of book shelves, the interior of the house was unaltered. The library occupied four rooms as indicated in the sketch plan.

Floor plans

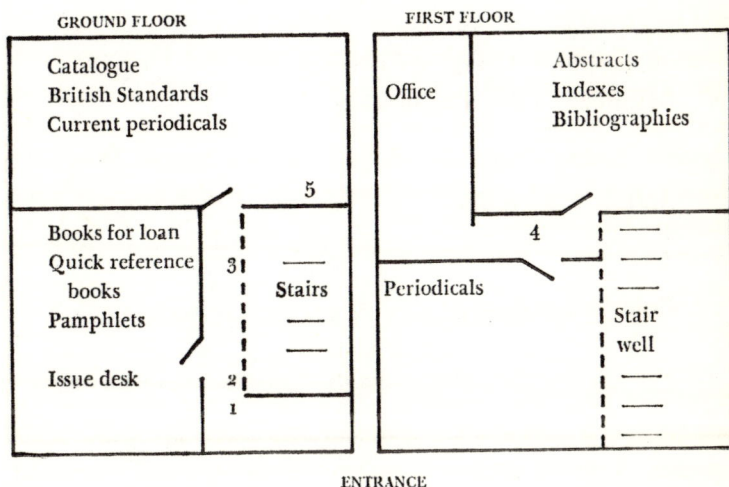

GROUND FLOOR

Catalogue
British Standards
Current periodicals

5

Books for loan
Quick reference
    books   3
Pamphlets   Stairs

Issue desk   2
                  1

FIRST FLOOR

Office

Abstracts
Indexes
Bibliographies

4

Periodicals

Stair
well

ENTRANCE

The positions of the guiding elements used are shown on the floor plans. The main items were:

1 *Main contents panel* set up on wall of entrance area.

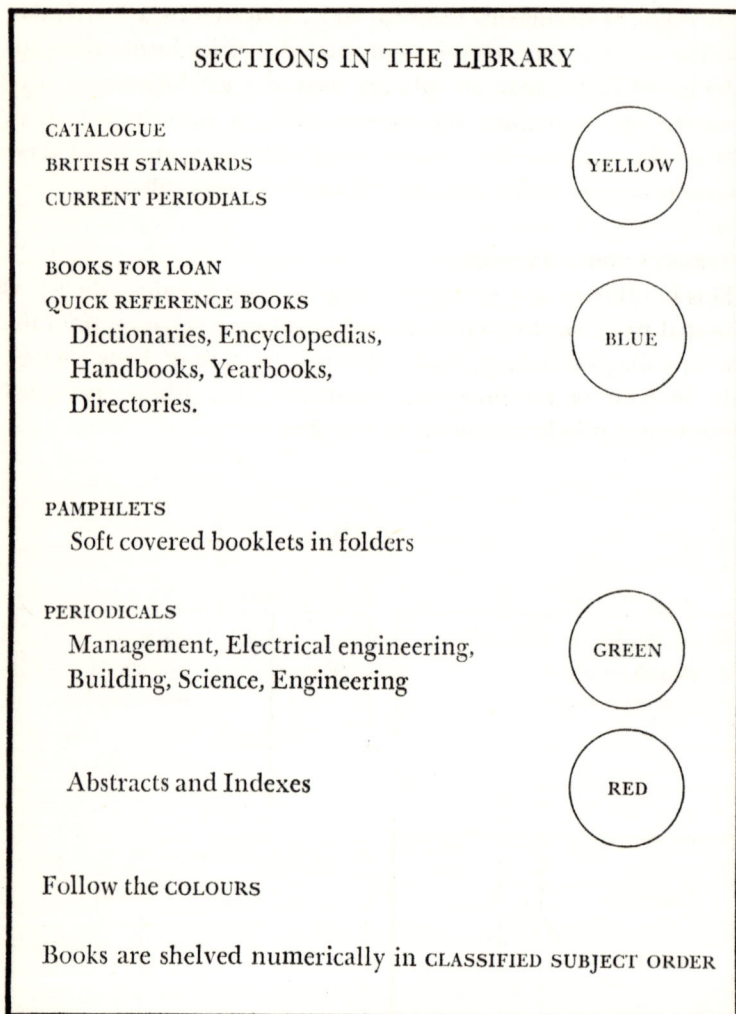

SECTIONS IN THE LIBRARY

CATALOGUE
BRITISH STANDARDS
CURRENT PERIODIALS

(YELLOW)

BOOKS FOR LOAN
QUICK REFERENCE BOOKS
  Dictionaries, Encyclopedias,
  Handbooks, Yearbooks,
  Directories.

(BLUE)

PAMPHLETS
  Soft covered booklets in folders

PERIODICALS
  Management, Electrical engineering,
  Building, Science, Engineering

(GREEN)

  Abstracts and Indexes

(RED)

Follow the COLOURS

Books are shelved numerically in CLASSIFIED SUBJECT ORDER

Hanging signs:

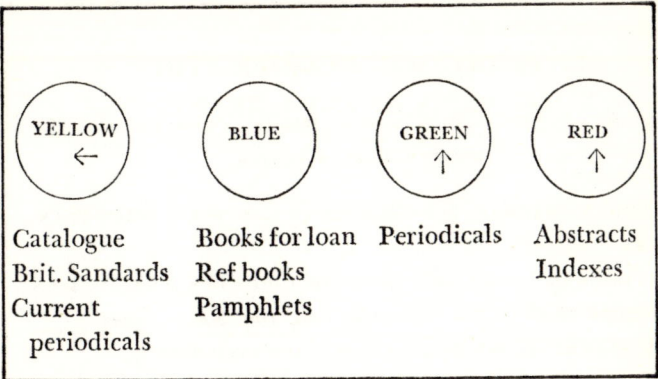

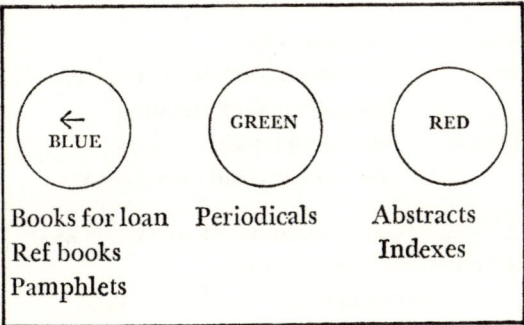

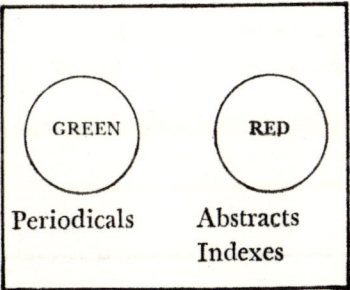

Each of the four main areas was indicated by an appropriately coloured signal fastened above the doorway.

DEWEY DECIMAL CLASSIFICATION

A LIBRARY CLASSIFICATION SCHEME MAKES EASIER THE SUBJECT ARRANGEMENT OF BOOKS

THE DEWEY DECIMAL CLASSIFICATION HAS FOUR MAIN PRINCIPLES:

1 WHOLE of KNOWLEDGE IS DIVIDED into TEN MAIN CLASSES represented by the NUMBERS 000, 100, 200 . . . 900;
2 Each MAIN CLASS is divided into TEN DIVISIONS;
3 Each DIVISION is DIVIDED into TEN SECTIONS;
4 Each SECTION may be SUB-DIVIDED by DECIMALS.

DEWEY DECIMAL CLASSIFICATION MAIN CLASSES:

000 GENERAL SUBJECTS	500 SCIENCES
100 PHILOSOPHY	600 APPLIED SCIENCES, TECHNOL
200 RELIGION	700 ARTS, ENTERTAINMENT
300 SOCIAL SCIENCES	800 LITERATURE
400 LANGUAGE	900 HISTORY and GEOGRAPHY

DEWEY DECIMAL CLASSIFICATION: EXAMPLE of a MAIN CLASS, SECTIONS and SUB-DIVISIONS:

MAIN CLASS	TECHNOLOGY	600
DIVISIONS	MEDICINE	610
	ENGINEERING	620
SECTION	MECHANICAL ENGNG.	621
SUB-DIVISIONS	ELECTRICAL ENGNG.	621.3
	ELECTRONICS	621.38

BOOKS IN THIS LIBRARY ARE ARRANGED NUMERICALLY IN ORDER OF THEIR DEWEY DECIMAL CLASSIFICATION NUMBERS.
That is in SUBJECT ORDER.

Instruction panel:

To complete the system a wall panel was set up in the area of the catalogue. The author and subject catalogues were on sheaves in loose leaf folders which were filed in pigeon holes. The subject index was kept on a revolving strip index fitting. As can be seen below, the instruction panel contained brief notes on the Dewey Decimal Classification scheme and some guidance in using the various sections of the catalogue.

USING THE LIBRARY CATALOGUE

THIS CATALOGUE records THE BOOKS, PAMPHLETS and PERIODICALS in this library so that they may be FOUND when required.

THE CATALOGUE has FOUR PARTS :

1 The AUTHOR catalogue. The book slips are filed in ALPHABETICAL order.
   NOTE : Some books do NOT HAVE AN AUTHOR.
   These are filed under TITLE.

2 The CLASSIFIED SUBJECT catalogue. The book slips are in NUMERICAL ORDER under DEWEY DECIMAL CLASSIFICATION NUMBERS.

3 The PERIODICALS catalogue. Periodicals are listed ALPHABETICALLY by TITLE.

4 The SUBJECT INDEX. The SUBJECTS covered by the CLASSIFIED SUBJECT CATALOGUE are listed ALPHABETICALLY with the DEWEY CLASSIFICATION NUMBERS. The SUBJECT INDEX is on a STRIP INDEX FILE.

If you know the AUTHOR of the book you need, use the AUTHOR CATALOGUE. If you want information on a SUBJECT, look for your SUBJECT in the SUBJECT INDEX. Find the CLASSIFICATION NUMBER and go to this NUMBER in the CLASSIFIED SUBJECT CATALOGUE.

This is the library of a polytechnic, which is on four floors in a new building. The general organisation of the library is based upon three subject departments and a general service department. Each subject floor is organised on a similar pattern and houses the books, the periodicals and the bibliographic aids relevant to the subject area. The classification scheme used by the library is the Universal Decimal Classification and the subject divisions are based upon the main classes of the UDC as follows: *Technology,* embracing books, journals and bibliographic aids covered by the UDC classes 6-799; *Science,* similar material for the UDC classes 5-599 and the *Humanities,* which is covered by UDC classes 0-399 and 8-999.

Each floor is roughly the same shape and dimensions and has a single entrance for readers. The entrance is at the south end of each room and is approached from a broad stairway with spacious landings. The guiding scheme follows a simple pattern at two levels. At the first level there is a broad analysis of the subjects and services available on the various floors, each of

Floor plan—Subject department

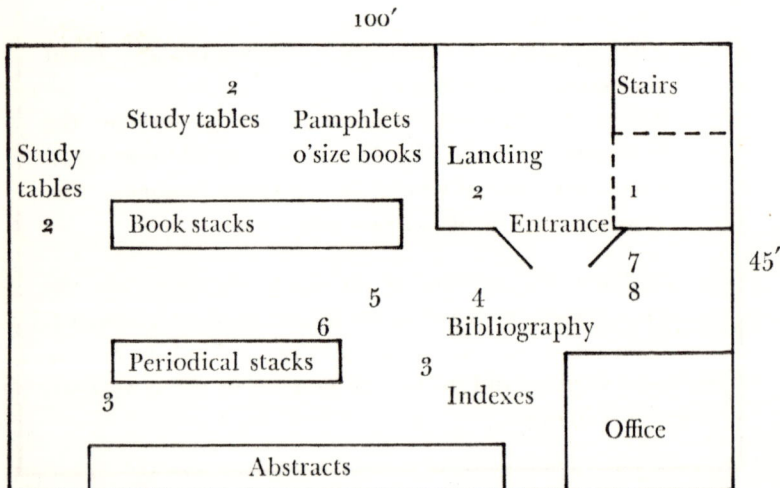

which is identified by a coding of coloured square signals. At the second level there is a more detailed analysis of books and services available on each of the four floors. The subject departments occupy one floor each, for Technology, for Science and for the Humanities. The departmental information is identified by coloured circular signals. A similar colour coding is used for documents and services on each of the four floors; namely, yellow circles for the catalogues, red for bibliographic aids, blue for periodicals, green for services and brown for library staff rooms.

The permanent visual information; wall panels, hanging signs, contents information used in the guiding scheme was as follows:

1 *Main contents panel*

SUBJECT DEPARTMENTS IN THE POLYTECHNIC LIBRARY

Follow the COLOURS

FLOOR			
2	TECHNOLOGY UDC 6-799 Medicine, Engineering, Management, Arts, Town Planning, Entertainments, Gramophone Records, Maps. County Technical Librarian.		RED
1	SCIENCE UDC 5-599 Mathematics, Computers, Physics, Chemistry, Geology, Biology. Library Class Room.		GREEN
MAIN	LOANS AND INFORMATION Main Catalogue, Reserved Text Books, Quick Reference Books, Periodicals (Current Year), British Standards. Hertis Information Service. Photocopying. Snack Bar.		BROWN
GRND	HUMANITIES UDC 0-399 8-999 Philosophy, Psychology, Sociology, Literature, Foreign Languages, Geography, History.		BLUE

This panel was set up outside the main entrance to the library and on each stair landing.

2 *Departmental contents panel*

SCIENCE   UDC 5-599

Sections in this department

GREEN

Follow the COLOURS

STAFF READING BOOK
Trade literature,
Foreign Standards
Report series,
Research organisations

GREEN

SUBJECT CATALOGUE
UDC 5-599
SUBJECT INDEX A-Z

YELLOW

PERIODICALS
Current seven years

BLUE

INDEXING/ABSTRACTING
PUBLICATIONS,
PAMPHLETS, OVERSIZE BOOKS

RED

OFFICES
LIBRARY CLASS ROOM

BROWN

This information is placed outside the entrance to the department. Reduced photographic copies of this panel have been set up at two positions in the study area.

INDEXING and ABSTRACTING PUBLICATIONS

(RED)

filed in HUMANITIES dept

(For complete list of these publications
received by this LIBRARY see PRINTED LIST)

Abstract Journal of Scientific & Technical In-
formation (USSR Referativnyi)
Aslib Book List
British Humanities Index
(Subject Index to Periodicals)
British National Film Catalogue
CBI Education & Training Index
CIRF Abstracts
Education Index
Express Information of Foreign Literature on
Library Science and Documentation
Express Information of Hungarian Literature
in Library Science and Documentation
Information Science Abstracts
(Documentation Abstracts)

Language Teaching Abstracts
Library of Congress Catalogue of Motion Pictures
Library and Information Science Abstracts
Library Literature
Library Science Abstracts
Psychological Abstracts
Research Index (Business Surveys)
Research in Education
Research into Higher Education Abstracts
Social Sciences & Humanities Index
Sociology of Education Abstracts

INDEXING/ABSTRACTING publications are aids to finding information published in PERIODICALS
etc
To use an INDEXING publication look under the appropriate SUBJECT HEADING
To use ABSTRACTING publications:
(a) In a SINGLE ISSUE consult the CONTENTS LIST
(b) In a COMPLETE VOLUME use the INDEXES
For more detailed guidance, use the INDEXING/ABSTRACTING INFORMATION STATIONS

This information is placed at the beginning and end of the stacks containing these indexes and abstracts in the Humanities Department. Similar information appears in the abstract areas of the other subject departments.

Hanging signs

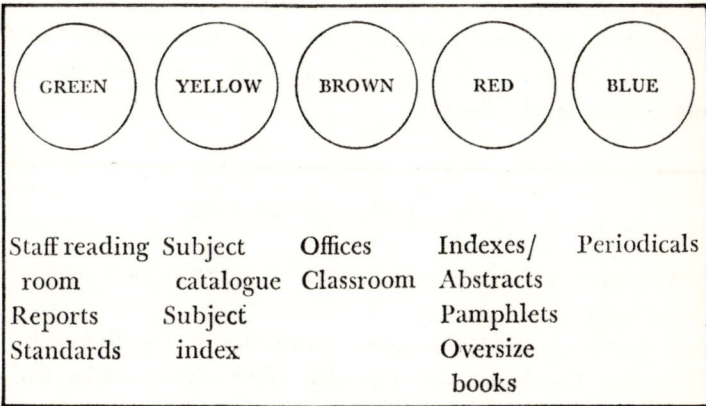

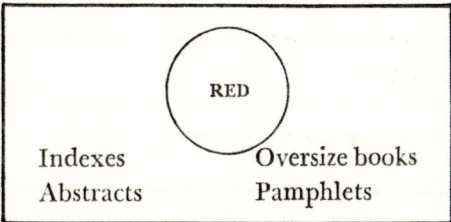

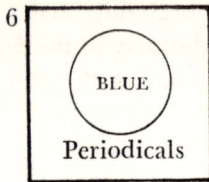

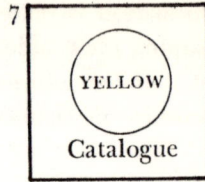

6 BLUE Periodicals

7 YELLOW Catalogue

8

A catalogue instruction panel was mounted on the wall above the catalogue cabinets. In each subject department a classified catalogue records the books and pamphlets in the department. Figure 4 shows the information included on one such panel. More detailed information including notes on the structure of the *Universal Decimal Classification* were placed over the main catalogue on the service floor.

USING THIS CATALOGUE

The CATALOGUE in this Department is a CLASSIFIED SUBJECT CATALOGUE.

(*ie* Cards are filed NUMERICALLY in order of UDC *Numbers.*) In this Catalogue are recorded ONLY those books and pamphlets with UDC NUMBERS:

5 -599

On the Catalogue Cabinet is a PRINTED SUBJECT INDEX. SUBJECTS are listed in ALPHABETICAL ORDER showing the UDC NUMBER used.

To USE THIS CATALOGUE, find your SUBJECT in the SUBJECT INDEX; note the CLASSIFICATION NUMBER used; and, go to this number in the CATALOGUE.

The COMPLETE CATALOGUE is on the MAIN FLOOR.

Figure 4

INFORMATION ON A CATALOGUE CARD

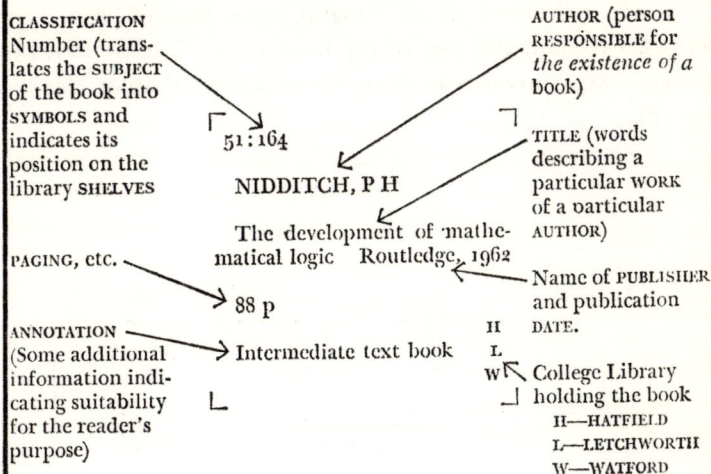

CLASSIFICATION
Number (trans-
lates the SUBJECT
of the book into
SYMBOLS and
indicates its
position on the
library SHELVES

AUTHOR (person
RESPONSIBLE for
the existence of a
book)

51 : 164

TITLE (words
describing a
particular WORK
of a particular
AUTHOR)

NIDDITCH, P H

The development of mathe-
matical logic   Routledge, 1962

PAGING, etc.

88 p

Name of PUBLISHER
and publication
DATE.

ANNOTATION
(Some additional
information indi-
cating suitability
for the reader's
purpose)

Intermediate text book

H
L
W   College Library
holding the book
H—HATFIELD
L—LETCHWORTH
W—WATFORD

For more DETAILED GUIDANCE in using the MAIN CATALOGUE
use the CATALOGUE INFORMATION STATION on MAIN FLOOR.

Figure 4 (contd)

LIBRARY GUIDING PATTERNS 3

This library catering for librarians, comprises a large ground
floor reading room and basement stack room. The general
arrangement places the most recent and most used books and
periodicals in the reading room while the older and less used
materials are shelved in the basement. A number of commercial
suppliers have deposited examples of library fittings, furniture
and materials which are on display at various positions in the
reading room and in the basement. The books and pamphlets in
the library have been classified, using two different classification
schemes, and there are two sequences of books in the shelves. The
catalogue is in three sequences: a printed catalogue for books
taken into the library up to 1956 and two sequences in a card

catalogue. The earlier sequences are classified by the Dewey Decimal Classification and the current sequence is classified using CRG (Classification Research Group) Classification. In this library, it was not convenient to use hanging signs. Instead ' flag ' signs were placed upon the tops of the book stacks. The construction of these ' flag ' supports is described in a later chapter (plate V nos 1, 7).

Floor plan

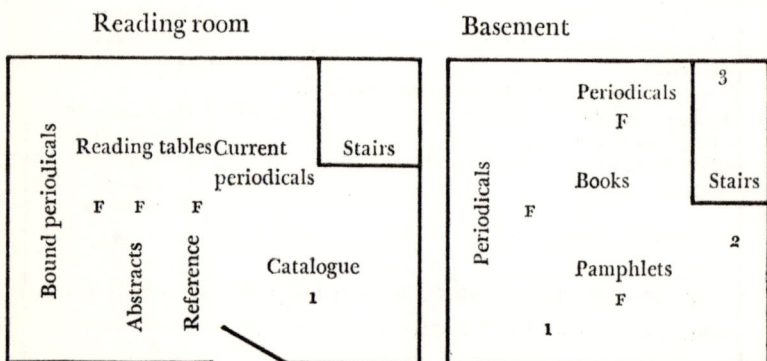

Reading room   Basement

Reading room panel:
Bound periodicals | Reading tables | Current periodicals | Stairs | F F F | Abstracts | Reference | Catalogue 1

Basement panel:
Periodicals F | 3 | Books | Stairs | Periodicals F | 2 | Pamphlets F | 1

The guiding elements included:

SECTIONS IN THIS LIBRARY

Please follow the COLOURS

Ground floor

CATALOGUE   (YELLOW)

PERIODICALS
  Current periodicals   (BLUE)
  Bound volumes

ABSTRACTS and   (RED)
  INDEXES

REFERENCE BOOKS   (BROWN)
  and STANDARD WORKS

Basement

PERIODICALS   (BLUE)
  In foreign languages
  In English

PAMPHLETS   (GREEN)
  and REPRINTS

BOOKS FOR LENDING   (BROWN)

DISPLAY MATERIALS   (ORANGE)
  (Various positions in the library)

This information was placed at the entrance to the library and repeated on the wall of the basement.

SECTIONS IN LIBRARY BASEMENT

PERIODICALS : FOREIGN LANGUAGE	BLUE *(square)*
ENGLISH LANGUAGE	BLUE *(circle)*
PAMPHLETS : Up to 1965 (DEWEY CLASSIFICATION)	GREEN *(circle)*
From 1966- (CRG CLASSIFICATION)	GREEN *(square)*
OVERSIZE (IN VERTICAL FILE) GREEN *(circle)*	GREEN *(square)*
BOOKS : Up to 1965 (DEWEY CLASSIFICATION)	BROWN *(circle)*
From 1966- (CRG CLASSIFICATION)	BROWN *(square)*
OVERSIZE BROWN *(circle)*	BROWN *(square)*
DISPLAY MATERIALS	ORANGE *(circle)*

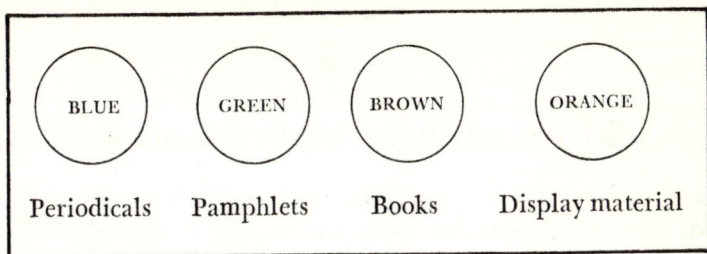

BLUE	GREEN	BROWN	ORANGE
Periodicals	Pamphlets	Books	Display material

'F' FLAG SIGNS

These replace the hanging signs which were used in the two previous examples. These signs were placed on top of the book stacks so that the identifying colour code and relevant information jutted out from the line of the stacks so as to be seen from a distance.

In this guiding scheme colour was used to indicate the type of document, while the shape of the signal indicated a time sequence for books and pamphlets and a language division for periodicals. Square brown signals identified the most recent books and pamphlets, brown circles the older material. In the periodicals blue circles identified those published in English and blue squares the periodicals in foreign languages.

3

Audio visual aids: information stations

THE PURPOSE OF THE visual information which was discussed in the last chapter was first to alert the reader to an understanding of the content and organisation of the library and, secondly, to save the time taken to find the required documents or services. In general the information supplied is the kind which is assimilated in seconds rather than minutes. For its effectiveness it relies somewhat on the advertising slogan techniques of keeping an idea alive. ' Beer is best ', ' Here is the catalogue ', ' Drink a pinta ', Here are the ' Reference books ', ' Pamphlets ', ' Oversize books '.

To the ordinary reader these ideas do not have an important place in his thoughts, and perhaps the most useful function of the library signs is to bring library thoughts to the surface of the reader's mind. When this library-directed thinking process has begun, some further detailed information can be communicated.

However, signs, instruction labels and similar devices can only carry very general incomplete information and it is necessary to have some means of supplying additional information to readers. What the reader wishes to know may be very straightforward. Where do I find a German dictionary? Do you have a copy of *Roget's thesaurus*? Or, the question may be rather specialised— how do I use *Science citation index*? On the other hand, the enquiry may be very complex—I want to find out what is known about drug addiction among factory workers in Britain? Where can I obtain information on mass production methods for manufacturing padlocks?

This additional help for readers can be supplied in several ways. The reader's first reaction is generally to ask a member of the library staff. For the reader needing a dictionary or a copy of *Roget,* anybody working in the library could supply the necessary service. The case of the person wanting to use *Science citation index* presents a different problem. First of all, this bibliographic aid is a difficult one for an inexperienced person to use, so that, for satisfactory guidance, the reader will need to contact a librarian who has the necessary experience and who also has some skill in giving instruction. Even in a college or university library, such qualified staff is frequently busy with other duties. The third type of query involves an even wider use of information sources and calls for both library time and staff expertise.

A second way of supplementing visual guidance and instruction is by the publishing of printed guides and other library literature. These publications are an essential part of any guiding programme; however, this aspect of library exploitation is considered in some detail in the next chapter. Yet a third way of making readers aware of how to find and use information has been through the provision of library tours and courses. This has been of special importance in college and university libraries, and the place of such courses in a guiding system will be discussed in some detail in a later section of the manual. The fourth way of supplementing visual guiding in a library is by means of various kinds of audio and visual devices, many of which are operated by the readers without assistance from the library staff. These aids are now familiar to many librarians. They include films, film strips, slides, tape recordings, closed circuit television and videotape recordings, in various combinations.

Such aids may be considered in two groups. The first contains material which is designed to tell readers about library matters and the use of information in general, without having a particular library in mind. The second group of aids has been produced in order to instruct readers in the use of one individual library, and may be regarded as an integral part of that library's guiding plan.

AIDS WITH GENERAL APPLICATION

Looking briefly at the first group of aids, these fall into three broad categories. Those which have the purpose of simply arousing an interest in books and libraries are mostly directed at children. Usually, these are films or film strips, and some examples are:

' Finding information ', an American film by Churchill Films and dated 1962. A small boy finds a ladybird, asks a friend what it is and goes on to the library to find out something more about ladybirds. This experience introduces the boy to libraries as a source of interest and enjoyment.

'And someting more ' is an American film made under the Knapp School Libraries Project. It deals with the place of a library in a primary school as an active part of the teaching programme. Children take part in the day-to-day running of the library and use not only its books but also films, slides and an overhead projector. The teachers hold book review sessions as part of their classes.

' Books go walkabout' is a Tasmanian film, describing the mobile library service from Hobart into its country districts. Visits are made to an old people's home, a beach camping site, several farms and a country school.

For American materials in this field there is an excellent annotated list[1] by Shirley L Hopkinson entitled *Instructional materials for teaching the use of the library*. It is dated 1971, so that some recent information is not included. The bibliography covers a wide range of material, incuding films, film strips, written guides and other miscellaneous aids. One section, for example, lists nine diagnostic and achievement tests which can be used to assess library skills.

The second category of general aids is that designed to explain a particular library service. Again, this type of aid is commonly a film. A good example of such a film is 'At your request ', produced by the National Lending Library for Science and Technology in Britain. The film first shows how the need for information can arise in industry, at a university, or in a research laboratory. It goes on to show something of the resources of the National Lending Library, and then describes the warehousing techniques used to provide a rapid interlibrary loan service. Although the subject matter relates to specialised information, the treatment of the subject gives the film a very wide general appeal. Unfortunately, this film is also ten years old and will soon be obsolete.

'The Medlars story' is a somewhat similar film, made by the National Library of Medicine at Bethesda in the USA, in 1963. This film describes how a computer system can be used to retrieve references to medical literature. Since the film was made, this service has greatly increased its scope. The computer tapes based upon the items recorded in *Index medicus* are now available for processing in Britain and other countries outside America.

'Library of Congress' was made in 1969. The film describes, first, the preparation of a report for a congressman. The subject chosen is 'The moon as a base for future space exploration', and the film explains how the various information specialists gather the necessary data. Next, the film shows how the library is used by a visiting professor who is preparing to write a biography of Francis Hopkinson; and, lastly, shows a scholar from a South American country who wishes to consult the Hispanic collection. The film ends with mention of some other special collections and a note on the work of the classification section of the library, the card service and the copyright activities.

'SBN 72' was made in Britain for a television series in 1972. The film describes how a computer is being used to compile a list of books published in Britain and how the concept of a *Standard book number* was developed by publishers and librarians working together. The film also shows how MARC (the machine readable catalogue) is produced; and explains the functions of the LASER (London and South Eastern Region) computerised union catalogue. Finally, some of the possible applications of LASER-type computerised catalogues, with bibliographical control through *Standard book numbers,* are discussed. These potentialities are illustrated by special reference to the experiments at Brighton Public Library.

Also within this general category of audio visual materials is an increasingly large number of aids of various kinds designed to give instruction in the use of specific publications, for example abstract services.

Several films and film strips dealing with the use of a library catalogue have been produced commercially. One film, also rather old, ' Library research in high school ', produced in 1959, includes guidance in the use of a dictionary card catalogue and a brief discussion of the structure of the Dewey Decimal Classification. Film strips are only useful as an aid, to be used with some kind of spoken commentary. A few titles are mentioned at the end of this chapter.

Lastly, in recent years a great deal of effort has been expended in producing tape recordings, usually supplemented by illustrative slides or printed charts, as an aid in explaining the use of specific bibliographic aids and the subject literature of various disciplines. The Massachusetts Institute of Technology Model Library Program has produced a series of tape recordings supported by ' handout sheets '. Details of this program appear at the end of the chapter. A somewhat similar series of aids is being produced under the auspices of SCONUL (Standing Conference of National University Libraries) by a group of university and college librarians in Britain. The tape recordings in this program are also listed at the end of the chapter.

The aids which we have discussed so far have been prepared to give instruction in the use of libraries and information with general application. Some are directed at children, some at college students and some at post-graduate and research personnel, but the instruction has not been related to a particular library or collection of literature. The group of audio visual aids which we now wish to consider are those designed to exploit the resources of a particular library.

AIDS FOR A SPECIFIC LIBRARY

Once again, various types of media may be employed for this purpose—films, tape recordings, tape and slide or tape and chart combinations, video tape recordings and closed circuit television. Moreover, these aids serve various purposes. A film or tape recording may be designed to take the place of a general tour of the library, or to supplement such a tour by giving the readers a broad view of the content and organisation of the library. An aid may also serve the more specialised purpose of giving readers instruction in the use of the catalogue and the classification scheme. Such aids may also be designed to show readers how to use individual publications such a bibliographies, periodicals indexes and abstracts. Whatever the medium, an introduction to the library sets out to tell readers what the library contains and how it is organised, why it has this particular type of organisation and where the major books and services are to be found. Sometimes brief instructions for the use of the catalogue are included with a note on the use of the reference books and the periodical indexes. Very many examples of films and other audio visual aids for this purpose have been reported in the library literature.

One of the earlier successful tape/slide combinations was made at a college library in London, where the librarian had a series of slides made to illustrate various working sections of her library. She then recorded on tape the information she wanted to go with each slide. In the library introduction program, students first heard the tape recording and saw the relevant slides in the classroom. They then visited the library where the tour followed almost exactly the program described in the tape recording. By this means the audio visual information supplied by the tape and slides was immediately reinforced by the practical experience in the library, where the students were able to see and use the catalogue and to find information in dictionaries, encyclopedias and other reference books.

An example of this reinforcement of audio information by another means was a film and printed guide combination made by the University of Illinois some ten years ago, entitled, ' Your library '. The film was directed at students preparing for a term essay. In the film, the students were taken to the library where they were introduced to its various services; shown how a book might be borrowed; how to use the catalogue; the kind of information to be found in the reference library, also, how to use the periodical indexes. They were shown something of the internal organisation of the library and its various departments and collections. The chief purpose of the film was to give life to information in a printed guide with the same title, ' Your library ', and which covered almost the same subject information as the film, although in much greater detail.

Some years ago, too, Southampton University Library in Britain made a very short film with the simple purpose of making students aware of the existence of the university library as a friendly and helpful place to go. Two students, a man and a girl, were depicted as walking casually through the library building. The girl was the more aware of library activity and pointed out the catalogue and other features in the library, but there was very little reference to the subject material or the information which could be found.

The Hatfield Polytechnic library was particularly fortunate in having a film made by professional film producers. The Central Office of Information made the film 'Automated library' for showing in an overseas television programme series 'This week in Britain '. The producer has kindly given permission to reproduce the script of the film which appears at the end of this chapter. In essence, you will see that the film has the special purpose of directing the attention of the library user to the various visual and other aids, which are permanently established in the library. The purpose of these aids is to help the reader to find the information or the service he wants with a minimum waste of time. In this case the filmed information is reinforced by the colour guiding and the permanent visual information set up in the library.

INFORMATION STATIONS

Let us now consider some of the ways of giving automatic instruction in the use of library facilities. The most important means of finding information in any library is, of course, the catalogue, so that an understanding of the principles behind the classification scheme and the ability to use the catalogue are essential for any serious library user. Mention has already been made of the published films and film strips which have been produced by commercial companies to explain the use of the catalogue and the classification. The weakness of these commercial productions is that the material does not relate particularly to the interests of the library and, therefore, of the readers in it. It is probably more effective to give instruction which relates to a particular catalogue and the classification as it is used in a particular library. Such specific aids should, of course, be as close as possible to the relevant books or services, and the audio visual facilities should be usable by a reader without reference to the library staff. They should also be available all the time that the library is open.

Ideally, the pre-recorded information will form a final stage in a system of instruction which is based upon permanent visual information. For example, over the catalogue, or standing on the catalogue cabinet, there will be a sign or panel setting out simple instructions for using each part of the catalogue. The pre-recorded information then becomes a direct extension of these instructions. In such an arrangement the catalogue complex includes the catalogue itself, clear printed instructions as to how to use it, contents information explaining exactly what is recorded in each part of the catalogue, and finally, an audio visual facility where the reader can receive individual instruction in a fairly detailed use of all parts of the catalogue, and an understanding of the principles behind the classification scheme and its application in the organisation of the library.

At this point, it may be worth while looking at some of the requirements and conditions for preparing audio visual aids of this kind. First of all it is necessary to remember that the voice in the recording is taking the place of a personal adviser who is communicating with a single reader. The language should therefore be simple, relaxed and informal. The tone should be friendly and the style conversational. It is usually unwise to assume that the reader understands very much about the subject, but it is necessary also to realise that the listener is an intelligent human being.

The next point to consider is the kind of person who is listening to the recorded voice. In some libraries the range of readership is very wide and there will be very great differences between individual readers with respect to their previous library experience. However, this type of aid is likely to be used mostly in academic or college libraries of one kind or another, and consequently there are not such very great differences between the needs of readers using such aids in those libraries. Having decided upon the kind of language and the level of previous experience of the reader, one librarian, who has been very successful in preparing aids of this kind, has suggested that the next stage is to list what are considered to be the most important requirements for the effective use of the catalogue or the indexing or abstracting service for which recorded instruction is to be prepared, and, having listed these most important features, to note down the questions that the reader should be able to answer after he has taken in the information in the recorded instruction.

Another factor which seems to be worth thinking about is the fact that audio information has comparatively little impact on a listener unless it is reinforced by some sort of visual information or experience. For this reason, pre-recorded instruction will need to be illustrated by charts or slides of various kinds. It is therefore necessary to decide what supporting information the tape recording is going to have; and whether colour is going to be used. Since an *information station* is part of the relevant library facility (*ie* the catalogue or the abstracts collections) and physically adjacent to it, the visual information needs to be related closely to the particular catalogue or publication, which the aid is designed to explain. Thus, the examples used as visual illustration will be directly related to the material which the reader has immediately at hand. This visual information, which may be photographic film in various forms or printed charts, serves several purposes. It may be used to reinforce spoken information. It can be used to illustrate spatial information and flow patterns, and lastly it can show sample pages or catalogue cards with annotation for clearer explanation of content and layout. If printed charts are used, a complete sequence of charts represents or summarises the content of the instruction provided by the aid and is therefore valuable in itself as a memory jogging device.

A further use of such charts is to provide a programmed exercise which can be used to extend and to illustrate the points covered by the recorded information.

TRANSMITTING AUDIO-VISUAL INFORMATION
IN THE LIBRARY

Most librarians will be acquainted with the better known devices for transmitting audio and visual information: tape recorders, head phones, television and videotape receivers, and the various film and slide projectors. However, there are three pieces of equipment which may be worth discussing briefly.

The first is a player/viewer booth designed at Surrey University, in Britain, which consists of a desk with a slightly inclined top. On the left is a glass screen underneath which is a carousel projector. On the right is a cassette tape recorder. Signals from the recorder are received either through head phones or from a loudspeaker. On the tape recording one track carries the instructor's voice, and a second track carries a signal which controls the operation of the slide projector, so that at the appropriate point in the instruction program the relevant slide is projected on to the screen. The program can be stopped by the operator at any point. This equipment was designed for use with the aids which are being prepared under the SCONUL scheme which has been mentioned earlier.

The second piece of equipment was described by O Bertrand Ramsay of the Department of Chemistry at Eastern Michigan University.[2] The equipment is similar to that designed by Surrey University, except that the viewing screen is 24 inches wide and the surface is vertical. More technical details of audio-visual equipment is included in chapter 6.

The third system or device which may be of interest is transmission by inductive loop. The writer has had considerable experience in using this device. The loop itself is essentially a loop or series of loops of wire which is substituted for the loudspeaker circuit in a tape recorder. The loop becomes an audio frequency aerial from which the signals are received by means of a headset receiver. Some mechanical details of inductive loop transmission are discussed in chapter 6. There are several advantages in using loop transmission for library instruction. Signals can be heard through the headset without disturbing other readers. The reader listening to the instruction can move about freely within the signal area and is not hampered by cords as would be the case with normal earphones. This can be a particularly useful feature when, for example, giving instruction in the use of the catalogue. The signal area can be large, embracing a whole large room, or confined to a small area. In practice the signal area can be controlled simply by setting a volume control, so that several loops may be used in a comparatively small area. They can be suspended from the ceiling on a frame, attached to a wall, or concealed beneath a desk or table top. The headset receiver is a little more expensive than simple earphones, but the loop costs only a few pence. Although a tape recorder is the most likely source of audio information in library instruction, an inductive loop can be used to transmit audio signals from any device which normally has its output through a loudspeaker or through earphones. Some examples are a television receiver, record player or the radio.

Before going on to consider some of the scripts and illustrations from aids used in working libraries, it may be helpful to consider what library instruction is designed to achieve and where audio visual aids fit in to the scheme. All library instruction is concerned with very simple ideas which may be effectively communicated to readers in different ways. Most readers, even in college and university libraries, use the library in a very simple or shallow way; to obtain a particular book, to browse during some spare time, or as a comfortable place to study. For such purposes the reader's needs can be satisfied without any deep understanding of library techniques; and, to such people the idea of library instruction has little significance. Professor Knapp, in the Monteith survey, showed conclusively that motivation for a wider library use in a university could only come from the needs of the teaching programme. From these experiences it follows that, in a system which includes adequate instruction panels, only a small proportion of readers will use, automatically, these audio visual aids. They are, however, a necessary part of the guiding system. Perhaps their most useful function is as an aid which can be used to satisfy readers' specific enquiries as in the example quoted above, ' How do I use *Science citation index*?'.

Something has already been said about the factors to be considered when preparing an aid for a specific group of readers— their educational background, previous library experience and subject requirements. We have also reviewed some of the basic requirements of the recorded instruction for using the catalogue, periodicals indexes and abstracts; defining the principles, structure and content, illustrating the points made by suitable examples; and, where necessary, reinforcing audio information by visual experience. The readers in each library will have different needs, and to each librarian one way of solving the problem will appeal more than another. Therefore, probably the most useful function which this manual can perform for working librarians will be to supply some details of aids used by different libraries. For this reason, the chapter ends with an analysis of five scripts of recorded talks and the relevant slides or charts.

EXAMPLES OF AUDIO-VISUAL AIDS USED IN WORKING LIBRARIES

1 RECORDED TALK

This talk was used in a college of further education in England. The students were mainly day-release boys and girls coming from local factories to work for technicians' certificates. There was also a small group of students studying for advanced levels in the General Certificate of Education in order to take university degrees or similar qualifications. At this college, emphasis is placed upon training for practical skills, so that the verbal ability of students was not generally high.

The purpose of the talk was to give a brief introduction to the problem of finding a book on a particular subject by using a subject index on cards. A second talk was prepared to give a similar introduction to the catalogue. The audio-visual facility comprised a tape player, the output of which was fed into an inductive loop suspended above the catalogue. The students received the information through an independent headset

53

receiver. From the script you will notice that the audio information was reinforced by practical use of the subject index and by reference to illustrations and printed information in a handout folder, ' What is the subject index for?' The script below is reproduced by permission of the author, John Parfitt, Librarian, Dacorum College of Further Education, Hemel Hempstead, England.

LOOKING FOR A BOOK ON YOUR SUBJECT

Talk begins in ten seconds. Talk begins in five seconds. Before I say something about the subject index and later on about the catalogue, I am going to count from one to ten so that you can turn the earphones up or down to suit yourself; OK? One, two, three, four . . . ten. Now I can get on with telling you about the subject index and catalogue.

This talk lasts about five minutes and is about the subject index, but if at any time you feel you have heard enough there is no need to listen to the whole thing through. I have started with the most important things first, so that if you only want to listen for a couple of minutes you will still have got most of what I want to say to you. The rest of it is subsidiary, so you get the most important bits first, and when you have had enough, just stop. Just take the earphones off and hand them back. Now, if someone came up to me and said let me show you how to use the library subject index, I expect my first reaction would be: Why should I bother? What good will it do me? So in case that would be your first reaction too, I am going to say why I think it is useful for you to know how to use this list, because that is what a subject index is; but, before I do that, let me show you what a subject index is for. Walk over to the drawers marked subject index (they are on the right hand side of the two blocks of catalogue dawers), and pull out any one of them, just take a look inside, and what do you see? Lots of cards, each one with the typewritten name of a subject on it; and on the right hand side a number. Just put your thumb in anywhere among the cards and look at a few, you will see what I mean, on the left hand side there is a subject heading like Electronics or Nursing, or Tennis, or Philosophy, and on the right hand side they have got a number like 621.381 or 610.73 or 100.

What does this mean? Well, for a start, you must have noticed that nearly all the books in the library have numbered labels on their backs. If you look at the picture in the folder called ' What is the subject index for?', you will see a picture of the books with labels on their backs. The numbers on the right hand side of the cards in the file that you are looking at, are the same as the numbers on the backs of the books, and the cards are in alphabetical order in the drawers. That means, of course, that you find cards for the subject, aeroplanes, badminton, cricket, in the drawers marked A, B, C, and x-rays, yachting and zoology, in the drawers marked X, Y, Z. Each card has got the name of the subject on the left and on the right hand side the number, that is on the spine of the book. To get from the subject you want to finding a book about it, you look for the subject card in its alphabetical drawer, make a note of the number, and walk over to the shelves. The books are put on the shelves in the order of the numbers. You will see on the end of each shelf a guide to the numbers of the books that are on the bank of shelves.

Now, I told you that I would tell you the most important things first; and now you know them. This process of getting from the subject that you want to the number where the books are filed and then to the shelves, is the single most important thing you can learn about the library, but I did say that I would tell you something about why you should take the trouble to use it. After all, the librarians are there to answer questions, aren't they? Well, I suppose there are really two reasons. First, the librarians may be busy helping someone else when you want to find a book on your subject, or you may be too shy to ask directly for what you want. So now you can find these things by way of the subject index. Secondly, most libraries of firms, colleges and universities, are indexed in the same sort of way, so if you make sure you know how to use this index, you will not have much trouble with any other. There are just a few minor things I ought to say. One is that you will find more than one card for some subjects. Open the drawer marked ' Subject index E ' for instance, and take a look at *Economics*. You see that there are quite a lot of cards that start with *Economics*, one behind the other. There is a drawing of them in the folder. So you see what I mean? Look at Subject Index E—*Economics* and behind that you find several different cards with several different numbers; this is important to remember, books on Economics may be at more than one place on the shelves, so that you need to make a note of all the numbers that have a bearing on what you want to know; so always look at a card or two in front and behind the one you first find and, if you get several numbers, make a note of them all.

Another point is, that you may not find a card at all in the subject index for the subject that interests you. That means that either we have not got any books on it, or the card is in another place under a slightly different word. You could, for example, look up Computers and find that the card was under Computing Machines instead. You have just got to be a bit clever, and if you don't find what you want at first, think of another way that the card may have been filed or labelled.

The third thing is, do not forget that as well as looking where you would naturally look first, on the lending shelves, you should look at the reference books also. A reference book might be useful, even though you could not take it out of the library. You notice where they are—there is a big sign hanging up with ' Reference books ' in red on it. Look, also, at the oversize books. Quite a lot of sporting books and art books get filed there because they are too big to go on the ordinary shelves; and, at the series of boxes marked Pamphlets; they are all in number order in just the same way as the books on the lending shelves. So, if you do not find anything among the lending books, you may find something in one of those other places; and then there are some books that are kept in the office for various reasons. Some are Open University reference books. You can still have a look at those, even if you are not taking the Open University courses, and then there are set textbooks that can only be borrowed for a short time, but they may be useful to you. There are also books that have been put on one side because they are needed for special courses, but you can look at any of these books by asking for them at the library desk. There is a list of them kept in a big grey folder on the counter that is marked ' books available on request '.

Well that's all about the subject index really.

2 INFORMATION STATION SCRIPT

This talk was used in the Humanities Department of a polytechnic library. The station was set up adjacent to the stacks holding the abstracts and periodical indexes. The equipment comprised a simple battery operated cassette tape recorder, the output of which was fed into an inductive loop concealed beneath a table top. Signals were received through an independent head set receiver as in the previous example. The station could be operated by readers without library staff assistance, and was available at all times. The students at the polytechnic were studying for degrees or similar qualifications.

FINDING INFORMATION IN ABSTRACTS AND PERIODICAL INDEXES

This information station has been set up so that you can have guidance in the use of indexing publications and abstracts whenever you need it. The information includes a tape recorded commentary illustrated by a book of charts. As each chart is introduced there is a pause for you to read it. Some pauses may be rather short but you can look again at the charts when the commentary has ended. You can, of course, stop the tape player if you wish especially to study a particular chart. Please adjust the level of signal in your receiver, using the volume control on the headset.

Indexing publications are short cuts to the information to be found in periodical articles and similar publications. The purpose of an indexing publication is to supply sufficient bibliographic detail to enable the original document to be traced when required.

Now please look at chart 1.

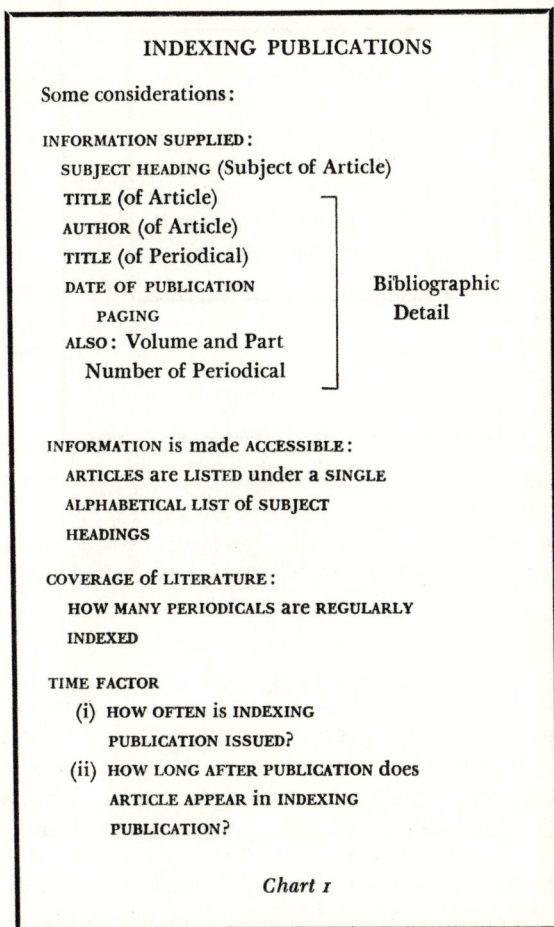

INDEXING PUBLICATIONS

Some considerations:

INFORMATION SUPPLIED:
  SUBJECT HEADING (Subject of Article)
  TITLE (of Article)
  AUTHOR (of Article)
  TITLE (of Periodical)
  DATE OF PUBLICATION   Bibliographic
     PAGING   Detail
  ALSO: Volume and Part
   Number of Periodical

INFORMATION is made ACCESSIBLE:
  ARTICLES are LISTED under a SINGLE
  ALPHABETICAL LIST of SUBJECT
  HEADINGS

COVERAGE of LITERATURE:
  HOW MANY PERIODICALS are REGULARLY
  INDEXED

TIME FACTOR
  (i) HOW OFTEN is INDEXING
     PUBLICATION ISSUED?
  (ii) HOW LONG AFTER PUBLICATION does
     ARTICLE APPEAR in INDEXING
     PUBLICATION?

Chart 1

PAUSE

Notice that the information is supplied under subject headings. The bibliographic detail includes the title of the article, the author of the article, and the title of the periodical where the original article was published, the date of publication and the paging. Sometimes the volume and part number of the periodical is also recorded. A typical example of an indexing publication is British Humanities Index.

Chart 2, please.

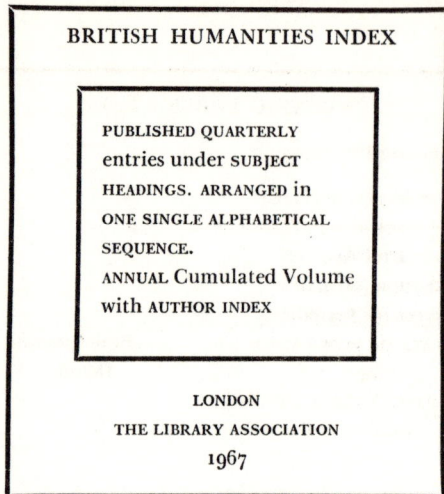

```
┌─────────────────────────────────────────────────┐
│                                                 │
│         BRITISH  HUMANITIES  INDEX              │
│                                                 │
│        ┌─────────────────────────────┐          │
│        │                             │          │
│        │   PUBLISHED QUARTERLY       │          │
│        │   entries under SUBJECT     │          │
│        │   HEADINGS. ARRANGED in     │          │
│        │   ONE SINGLE ALPHABETICAL   │          │
│        │   SEQUENCE.                 │          │
│        │   ANNUAL Cumulated Volume   │          │
│        │   with AUTHOR INDEX         │          │
│        │                             │          │
│        └─────────────────────────────┘          │
│                                                 │
│                                                 │
│                    LONDON                       │
│            THE LIBRARY ASSOCIATION              │
│                     1967                        │
└─────────────────────────────────────────────────┘
```

Chart 2

PAUSE

British humanities index is published quarterly. There is also an annual volume which contains information published in four quarterly issues.

Chart 3, please.

PAUSE

This shows a sample page from the quarterly issue of *British humanities index*. Note the article by Nigel Calder. Here you can see the kind of information recorded in *British humanities index*: The subject heading for the article is ' Computers '. The title of the article is ' Brains versus computers: how much decision making can we leave to the machine?'. The author of the article is ' Nigel Calder '. The title of the periodical where the original article was published *New statesman,* the date of publication 17th May 1968, and the paging p 645-648. There is often, also, details of the volume and part number of the periodical. The number ' 75 ' refers to volume 75 of the *New statesman*. On this chart, also, you will see examples of cross references and related headings. Information dealing with composers is recorded in the *British humanities index* under the subject heading ' Musicians ', and if you are interested in the subject Compensation at Law you may find useful information under the subject heading ' Injuries '.

Chart 4, please.

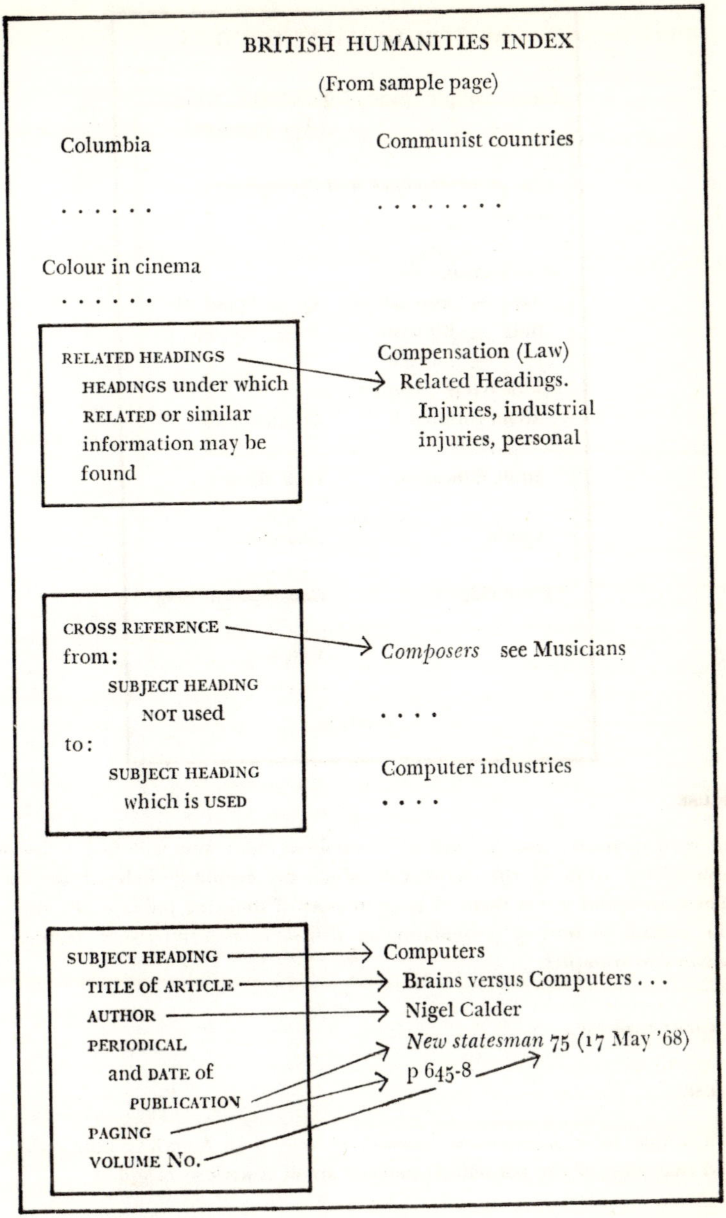

BRITISH HUMANITIES INDEX

(From sample page)

Columbia   Communist countries

. . . .

Colour in cinema

. . . . . .

RELATED HEADINGS   Compensation (Law)
    HEADINGS under which   → Related Headings.
    RELATED or similar   Injuries, industrial
    information may be   injuries, personal
    found

CROSS REFERENCE   → *Composers*   see Musicians
from:
        SUBJECT HEADING   . . . .
            NOT used
to:
        SUBJECT HEADING   Computer industries
            which is USED   . . . .

SUBJECT HEADING   → Computers
TITLE of ARTICLE   → Brains versus Computers . . .
AUTHOR   → Nigel Calder
PERIODICAL   → *New statesman* 75 (17 May '68)
    and DATE of
        PUBLICATION   → p 645-8
PAGING
VOLUME No.

Chart 3

```
┌─────────────────────────────────────────┐
│                                         │
│        BRITISH  HUMANITIES  INDEX        │
│                                         │
│   From  Sample  page — QUARTERLY  ISSUE  │
│                         (Apr-June 1968)  │
│                                         │
│   (LIST of PERIODICALS and Newspapers    │
│   indexed)                               │
│                                         │
│   ABBREVIATIONS USED                     │
│      Ass  = Association   Q = Quarterly  │
│      Bull = Bulletin      R = Review     │
│      J    = Journal                      │
│   List of TITLES (Approx 350):           │
│      Adam Internat R       Country Life  │
│      . . . . .             . . . . .     │
│      Adult Education       Folk Music J  │
│      . . . . .             . . . . .     │
│      Apollo                Guardian      │
│      . . . . .             . . . . .     │
│      Cambridge Q           Geographical Mag │
│      . . . . .             . . . . .     │
│                            Times         │
│                            . . . . .     │
│                  Chart 4                 │
│                                         │
└─────────────────────────────────────────┘
```

PAUSE

In each quarterly issue of *British humanities index* you will find a list of abbreviated titles of the periodicals which are regularly indexed therein. There are about 350 of them. A large number of indexing publications follow the general pattern of presentation of *British humanities index*. Here are one or two examples.

Chart 5, please.

PAUSE

Notice that *Social sciences and humanities index* is an American publication, and that most of the periodicals indexed are of American origin.

Chart 6, please.

```
┌─────────────────────────────────────────────────┐
│                                                 │
│   SOCIAL SCIENCES AND HUMANITIES INDEX          │
│        (from cover for March 1970)              │
│                                                 │
│        ┌───────────────────────────────┐        │
│        │                               │        │
│        │  QUARTERLY ISSUES             │        │
│        │        with                   │        │
│        │  CUMULATED ANNUAL VOL.        │        │
│        │  INDEXES 200 PERIODICALS      │        │
│        │  (largely of AMERICAN origin) │        │
│        │  INFORMATION under            │        │
│        │  ALPHABETICAL LIST of         │        │
│        │  SUBJECTS                     │        │
│        │                               │        │
│        └───────────────────────────────┘        │
│                                                 │
│        THE H W WILSON COMPANY                   │
│           New York USA                          │
│                                                 │
│              Chart 5                            │
│                                                 │
└─────────────────────────────────────────────────┘


    ┌────────────────────────────────────────┐
    │                                        │
    │      BRITISH TECHNOLOGY INDEX          │
    │                                        │
    │           (from cover)                 │
    │                                        │
    │     ┌──────────────────────────┐       │
    │     │                          │       │
    │     │  ENTRIES for ONE MONTH   │       │
    │     │  CUMULATED ANNUAL VOL    │       │
    │     │  SINGLE ALPHABETICAL     │       │
    │     │  SEQUENCE                │       │
    │     │                          │       │
    │     └──────────────────────────┘       │
    │                                        │
    │        LIBRARY ASSOCIATION             │
    │                                        │
    │             Chart 6                    │
    │                                        │
    └────────────────────────────────────────┘
```

PAUSE

British technology index is a companion index to *British humanities index*. It is published monthly with an annual volume.

Chart 7, please.

PROBLEMS IN USING INDEXING PUBLICATIONS

i   SUBJECT HEADINGS
    INDEXING PUBLICATION may NOT USE
    the SAME TERM for the SUBJECT as the
    person seeking information
    eg ATOMIC ENERGY for NUCLEAR
        ENERGY.

ii INDEXING PUBLICATION may record
    information under a BROADER SUBJECT
    under a DIFFERENT MAIN HEADING
    or an INVERTED HEADING
    eg ' COMPARATIVE RELIGION ' under
        ' RELIGION, Comparative ',
        ' COMPOSERS ' under ' MUSICIANS '

iii INFORMATION may be approached in
    DIFFERENT WAYS
    eg INFORMATION about ' COMPENSATION '
        under: ACCIDENTS, INJURIES.
        INFORMATION ON COMMUNICATIONS
        under: TELEPHONES, RADIO.

    ALWAYS CHECK: CROSS REFERENCES,
    RELATED HEADINGS AND ' SEE ALSO '
    REFERENCES

    TYPE of ORIGINAL PUBLICATION
    (a) PERIODICAL ARTICLES (most common)
        TITLES of PERIODICALS usually
        ABBREVIATED
    (b) REPORT SERIES
        Sometimes difficult to identify
    (c) CONFERENCE PAPERS (PREPRINTS)
    (d) PATENT SPECIFICATIONS

    WHEN in doubt CHECK LIST of TITLES of
    PERIODICALS INDEXED (in ANNUAL VOLUME)

Chart 7

This chart lists some of the commoner difficulties which crop up when using indexing publications. You may like to refer back to this information when this talk has ended.

Let us now look at some abstracting publications.

The purpose of an abstracting publication is to supply sufficient bibliographic detail to enable the original document to be traced when required, and to supply a summary or abstract of the subject content of the article to help the reader to decide whether he or she needs to read the original article.

Chart 8, please.

ABSTRACTING PUBLICATIONS

SHORT CUTS to INFORMATION in :
    PERIODICAL ARTICLES, REPORTS,
    CONFERENCE PROCEEDINGS, PATENT
    SPECIFICATIONS and sometimes in
    BOOKS.

SUBJECT COVERAGE
    USUALLY in a NARROWER SUBJECT
    FIELD than INDEXING PUBLICATIONS

INFORMATION SUPPLIED :
    TITLE (of ARTICLE, REPORT, etc)
    AUTHOR (of ARTICLE, etc)
    NAME of PERIODICAL, etc, (where
        ARTICLE was PUBLISHED)
    DATE of PUBLICATION
    PAGING
        ALSO SOMETIMES : VOLUME no and
        PART no of PERIODICAL
    WITH in ADDITION :
    An ABSTRACT or SUMMARY of the SUBJECT
        CONTENT (of the ARTICLE, etc)

ACCESSIBILITY of INFORMATION :
    In SINGLE ISSUES use CONTENTS LIST
    In COMPLETE VOLUME use SUBJECT
    INDEX

Chart 8

Notice that abstracts usually cover a wider range of publications, but deal with a narrower subject field. The bibliographic detail is the same as for indexing publications but an abstract is added. The arrangement, or accessibility, of information is different. Abstracts are numbered and in a single issue you need to use a contents list while in a complete volume there is an index. A fairly typical example of an abstracting publication is *Psychological abstracts*.

Chart 9, please.

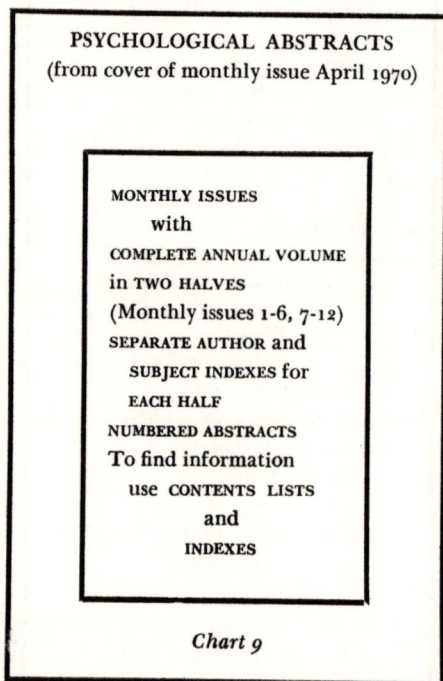

PSYCHOLOGICAL ABSTRACTS
(from cover of monthly issue April 1970)

MONTHLY ISSUES
with
COMPLETE ANNUAL VOLUME
in TWO HALVES
(Monthly issues 1-6, 7-12)
SEPARATE AUTHOR and
SUBJECT INDEXES for
EACH HALF
NUMBERED ABSTRACTS
To find information
use CONTENTS LISTS
and
INDEXES

Chart 9

PAUSE

You will notice that *Psychological abstracts* is issued monthly with an annual volume in two halves which includes subject and author indexes.

Chart 10 please.

From sample page

(PSYCHOLOGICAL ABSTRACTS)

Programmed Learning

6173

Knans William J
   An experimental study

. . . .

          6181

           . . .

          6182

          6183 . .

BIBLIOGRAPHIC DETAIL:	
AUTHORS (of article) →	Brien, E P Barrett, G et al
TITLE of article →	Uses of questionnaire in job evaluation.
Title of PERIODICAL →	*Journal of industrial psychology*
DATE of PUBLICATION →	1965, 3(4) 91-94
PAGING →	

Chart 10

PAUSE

This chart shows a page from *Psychological abstracts*. You will note that each abstract is serially numbered. The abstracts on this page are numbered 6171 to 6184.

   The bibliographic detail is exactly similar to that given in an indexing publication, but in addition to the bibliographic detail, there is an abstract or summary of the subject content of the article indexed. The information in the abstract helps the reader to decide whether or not to read the original article.

   Chart 11, please.

From sample page

PSYCHOLOGICAL ABSTRACTS

SUBJECT INDEX

Item . . . . . .   Job Performance

Japan . . . . .   Job Evaluation
      and performance evaluation
      executives   6225
      merit rating   6208

Jen . . . . .   Position description questionnaire
      versus joint rating system 6183

Chart 11

PAUSE

This chart shows part of the subject index for the 1967 volume of *Psychological abstracts*. In the subject index, under the subject ' Job evaluation ' we find indexed abstract no 6183.

Chart 12, please.

From sample page

(PSYCHOLOGICAL ABSTRACTS)

List of periodicals and other publications
represented in VOL 42 issues 1-6

Academic therapy
quarterly   . . . . .

      Cahiers de
      psychologie

Australian journal
of psychology   . . . . . .
. . . .

Chart 12

Finally, you will see that each complete volume of *Psychological abstracts* includes a list of full titles of periodicals regularly abstracted.

Now, there are a very large number of abstracting publications that follow generally the pattern of presentation in *Psychological abstracts*.

The Hatfield Polytechnic library holds a wide range of abstracting publications. On the shelf in front of you, you will see a guide to the indexing and abstracting publications received in this library. Notice that there is a subject index at the back.

Now look at chart 13, please.

PROBLEMS IN USING ABSTRACTING PUBLICATIONS

IN SINGLE ISSUES :

   A CONTENTS LIST indicates a BROAD SUBJECT GROUPING

   ABSTRACTS are NUMBERED

  Within the SUBJECT GROUP, ARRANGEMENT may be

     (a) A CLASSIFIED ONE under SUB-DIVISIONS

     (b) RANDOM under each BROAD SUBJECT

IN COMPLETE VOLUMES :

  There is usually a SUBJECT and AUTHOR INDEX

  SUBJECT INFORMATION may be

    Under a DIFFERENT SUBJECT TERM to the one

     used by the SEARCHER

    Under a BROADER SUBJECT or INVERTED HEADING

     eg ' COMPARATIVE RFLIGION ' under ' RELIGION

      COMPARATIVE '

       ' COMPOSERS ' under the BROADER term

      ' MUSICIANS '

  INDEXED INFORMATION refers back to NUMBERED ABSTRACTS

  Look for SPECIAL INSTRUCTIONS supplied by PUBLISHER

KEYWORD INDEXES :

  Prepared with the aid of a computer and based upon SIGNIFICANT

  WORDS in the TITLES of articles, of reports, etc

TYPES OF ORIGINAL PUBLICATION :

   1 PERIODICALS ARTICLES (TITLES of periodicals usually ABBREVIATED)

   2 REPORT SERIES (ABBREVIATED difficult to IDENTIFY)

   3 CONFERENCE PAPERS (including PREPRINTS)

   4 PATENT SPECIFICATIONS

   5 Sections from PUBLISHED BOOKS

   CHECK FIRST List of TITLES of PERIODICALS, etc

     ABSTRACTED (often in each ANNUAL VOLUME)

Chart 13

This chart summarises the problems of using abstracting publications. You may like to look at it again when the talk is finished. You will find on the shelf in front of you an example of a keyword index.

Chart 14, please.

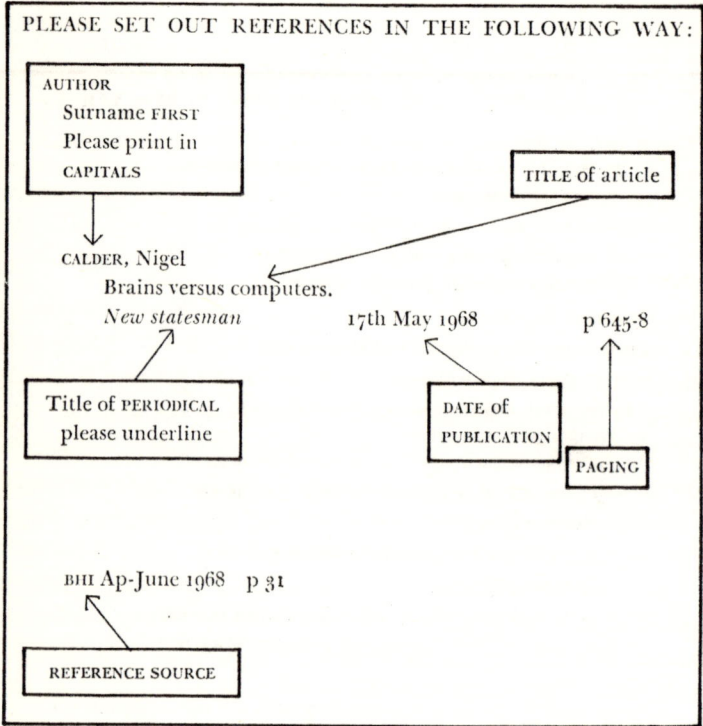

Chart 14

PAUSE

The purpose of using indexing and abstracting publications is to record references. Some of these references you will have to borrow from a distant library. If you write down all references as shown on this chart, you will be sure of obtaining them with the minimum delay. The habit of printing the surnames of authors can save a great deal of time. When checking back on information, there is no clue to the spelling of a hastily written author's name. On the other hand, there will be little difficulty in guessing the words of a title.

From the searcher's point of view, it is worth while recording the source of abstracted information, *eg British humanities index,* April to June 1968 p 31. If you wish to look again at the reference, checking back is very simple when this information is recorded.

This is the end of this brief introduction to the use of indexing and abstracting publications, but the only way to understand these short cuts to information is to use them in a practical situation, and following chart 14 is a short exercise which will give you the opportunity to do this. You will need a sheet of the working paper which is provided on the shelf in front of you.

Thank you for listening. Please switch off your head phones and the tape recorder. Please also rewind the tape so that it will be ready for the next user of the information station.

3 TAPE RECORDING WITH ANNOTATED SAMPLE PAGES

The script of *Science citation index* was composed, and the display units were fabricated, for use in the MIT Barker Engineering Library, as part of the activities of the Model Library Project of Project Intrex at Massachusetts Institute of Technology, Cambridge, Massachusetts, USA. The Model Library Project was funded under a grant from the Council on Library Resources Inc, Washington, DC. The text (below) and the photographs of display units are reproduced by kind permission of the Project Director.

The audio information in this program is transmitted from an endless tape cassette player, and is received through a telephone handset receiver. In a later chapter this equipment is described more fully. The visual material consists of a sample page from three indexes from *Science citation index* (1 *Citation index;* 2 *Source index;* 3 *Permuterm index*). On the sample pages the information referred to in the script is underlined in red.

SCIENCE CITATION INDEX SCRIPT

This tape runs for about five minutes and is supplemented by the notebook located in front of you. The notebook contains sample pages from *Science citation index* which illustrates the points discussed in this tape. We will direct you to the proper examples at the time you should refer to them.

69

Science citation index is a non-traditional reference tool for literature searching by author and subject. Its coverage is extensive and multidisciplinary, including journal articles in the engineering, physical, and social sciences. It is published every three months and cumulated annually and at five-year intervals.

Science citation index consists of five special indexes: the *Citation index, Source index, Permuterm index, Corporate index, and Patent index.* We'll discuss only the citation, source and permuterm indexes, which are the most frequently used.

To begin a subject literature search in the *Citation index,* you must know the author and other bibliographic details of at least one pertinent journal article. For example, if you wanted to do a search on the Mossbauer effect, you should know—beforehand—that this phenomenon was initially described by R L Mossbauer in a 1958 article published in *Zeitschrift für physik,* volume 151.

Turn to page 1 of the notebook for a demonstration of how the *Citation index* works, using the Mossbauer effect as the subject of interest. Look in column 2 at the cited-author entry for R L Mossbauer. Below the author's name, you'll find the last two digits of the years in which Mossbauer's articles were published. There is a listing for the 1958 article from *Zeitschrift für physik,* volume 151, page 124. This bold-type entry is the *cited* reference. It's immediately followed by an indented listing of author entries in regular type. These are the citing references. They tell you where and by whom the basic Mossbauer effect article was cited as a reference. The information for each of the sources includes—reading from left to right—the citing author's last name and initials, such as D E Carlson; the abbreviated source journal title, *Physics letters; Section A*; a coded indication for the type of source item, in this case ' L ' for ' letter '; the source journal volume number, A-29; the page in the source journal on which the citing article begins, 449; and finally, 69, the last two digits of the year in which the source journal was published. Codes and abbreviated journal titles are completely spelled out in the front pages of the first *Source index* of any volume of any year.

After you have found this list of citing references, you can determine their relevance by obtaining their complete titles from the *Source index.* Turn to sample page 2. Look at the entry for the article by D E Carlson from *Physics letters; Section A*—the same article which cited Mossbauer's article. The entry includes the author's name followed by the full title of the article. On the line following the title is the abbreviated journal title, the journal volume, the page on which the article begins, the year of the journal, the code ' L ' for ' letter ', the total number of references in the article, and the issue number of the journal, 8.

Finally, since 1968, a *Permuterm index* to the source articles has been published. This indexes articles by coupling significant words appearing in titles and subtitles. Turn to sample page 3. Look at the word ' Mossbauer '. Beneath it are indented listings of co-terms. Included as a co-term is the word ' effect '. Listed below the word ' effect ' are author's surnames and initials. By taking this information to the *Source index* you can locate all the information needed to fully identify the articles which have the words ' Mossbauer ' and ' effect ' in their titles.

For any additional questions on the use of *Science citation index,* refer to the detailed instructions on the inside front cover of each volume, or—of course—you may ask a librarian for help. We hope this tape will help get you started.

We'd appreciate it if you'd take a moment to fill out the questionnaire in the green notebook. Thanks for listening.

Please hang up the phone and the program will stop automatically.

4 TAPE RECORDING WITH SYNCHRONISED COLOURED SLIDES S1-S50

This script (and its accompanying coloured slides) were prepared under the SCONUL co-operative programme at Salford University by Miss A E Lumb and Dr O Meth-Cohn and is reproduced here by kind permission of the University Librarian.

A BASIC GUIDE TO THE USE OF BEILSTEIN: SCRIPT

S1 Title
This presentation is intended for those of you who have never used Beilstein's *Handbuch* and who are a bit scared by its size and apparent complexity, and by the fact that it is in German.

S2 Volumes of Beilstein
It is really very straightforward to use and requires only an elementary knowledge of German, plus a few basic rules about its organisation.

S3 Volumes of Beilstein
Beilstein's *Handbuch der organischen chemie,* commonly referred to as *Beilstein,* is a comprehensive work describing every organic compound known up to the time of its publication.

S4 Volumes of Beilstein and supplements
It was first issued in 1883 in two volumes by Friedrich Konrad Beilstein but has now reached its fourth edition and this is the one you should use.

S5 Cover title: Beilstein, 4th ed
It is arranged in sections, each covering a period of years, and each sub-divided according to a carefully devised classification scheme.

S6 Bound volumes of main work

The main work or ' Hauptwerk ' consists of thirty one volumes, which cover all organic compounds published up to the end of 1909; about one hundred and forty thousand in all.

S7 Bound volumes of first supplement

The first supplement or ' Erstes Ergänzungswerk ', which in the set shown here is identical in binding and colour to the main work, extends the coverage to 1919. Each volume of this supplement covers the same types of compounds as the main work.

S8 Close-up of spine of volume

The contents of each volume are indicated on the spine. Here are the volumes of the main work relating to isocyclic compounds.

S9 Bound volumes of second supplement

The same arrangement is employed in the second supplement or ' Zweites Ergänzungswerk ', which takes you up to 1929.

S10 Bound volumes of third supplement

The third supplement or ' Drittes Ergänzungswerk ', which extends the coverage to 1949 and which is still in progress; hence the variation in volume colour which you see here.

S11 Reader consulting Beilstein at table

To show you how to find your way around this vast amount of chemical information, let us now take a couple of examples. The first will show you how to trace a compound by its formula, and the second how to trace a compound by its name only.

S12 Structural formula for $C_7H_7ClN_2O_2$

Say you are interested in the chemistry of chloronitrotoluidines, and, in particular, you want to know about this isomer.

S13 Spine of subject index (close up)

First you look in the latest cumulative indexes, which are volumes 28 and 29 of the second supplement. There are two indexes to choose from, the subject index or ' Sachregister ' and

S14 Spine of formula index (close up)

the formula index or ' Formelregister '. As the compound you are interested in could have several names, it is better to consult

S15 Title page of vol 1 of formula index
the formula index, which you will find in volume 29. The formulae are arranged with carbon and hydrogen first, and then the other elements in alphabetical order. This is called the Hill system.

S16 Page 286 of formula index, E II 29 (whole page)
Here is the relevant section, and although the nomenclature is not always the one you are used to, it is usually straightforward once you know the system.

S17 Structural formulae of 5-chloro-2-nitro-2-nitro-4-methyl-aniline and 3-chloro-6-nitro-4-methyl-aniline
Your compound is a chloro-nitro-methyl-aniline, which suggests the name 5-chloro-2-nitro-4-methyl-aniline or 3-chloro-6-nitro-4-methyl-aniline.

S18 Page 286 of formula index (close up). Pencil points to compound.
The first name is, in fact, used in the formula index.

S19 Page 286 of formula index. Pencil points to volume number.
In the entry, the number in bold type, 12, gives the number of the volume in which the compound appears, both in the main work and the supplements. It is followed by the page number, 1007, in the main work. The roman figures I and II refer to the corresponding entries in the first and second supplements and the relevant pages, 441 and 537, follow the supplement numbers.

S20 Page 1007, vol 12, main work. Pencil points to compound.
You can now look up the entry in the main work, which you see here.

S21 Page 441, vol 12, first supplement. Pencil points to compound.
There is a corresponding entry on page 441 of the first supplement.

S22 Page 537, vol 12, second supplement. Pencil points to compound.
There is a corresponding entry on page 537 of the second supplement.

S23 Page 1007, vol 12, main work (close up). Pencil points to compound.
The entry for this compound in the main work is typical of many. First it gives its various names, then its empirical formula and structure. This is followed by the various methods by which the compound may be prepared.

S24 Page 1007, vol 12, main work. Pencil points to ' B '
The abbreviation ' B ' stands for formation. Usually a preferred method of preparation is also given. Then follow the physical, chemical and physiological properties.

73

3*

S25 Page 1007, vol 12, main work. Pencil points to ' F '
Melting points are prefixed by the letter ' F ' and boiling points by ' Kp ',
with the relevant pressure as subscript.

S26 Table of abbreviations. Pencil points to ' B ' and ' F '
You will find a table of abbreviations at the beginning of the volume. Finally,
any derivatives and significant reactions of the compound are noted.

S27 Page 1007, vol 12, main work. Pencil points to references (Claus, Bocher)
Relevant references to the data are usually given in the form: author,
abbreviated journal title, volume number and page number, but the year is
frequently left out. The abbreviation of the journal title is often not the
commonly accepted one, but both the year and the title can be found in the
tables at the front of the appropriate volume.

S28 Page 1007, vol 12, main work. Pencil points to 'A'
Thus 'A' stands for *Leibig's annalen der chemie, and the bold number in*
the entry indicates the volume number, 265.

S29 Table of years corresponding to volume numbers
This corresponds in the table of years, which you will also find at the beginning of the volume to the year 1891.

S30 Same as S29 in close up. Pencil points to 1891

S31 German-English dictionaries. Example on table
A good German-English chemical dictionary, such as *Patterson,* will often
help you when consulting Beilstein. For example, you may come across the
problem of German popular names for organic compounds, which are unfamiliar to the English-speaking chemist. Common functional groups also
have their own names in German.

S32 Word, ' Säuere '
Thus an acid is known as a ' Säure '. So if you wish to look up the chemistry
of cycloheptane-carboxylic acid, for instance

S33 Page 742, subject index, E II 28 (close up). Pencil points to cycloheptan-
carbonsäure
The subject index entry in *Beilstein* will be ' Cycloheptan-carbonsäure ' and
as in the first example, you are referred to entries in the appropriate volume,
in this case volume 9. Thus in the main work you will find the entry on
page 12, in the first supplement on page 7 and in the second supplement on
page 9.

S34 Page 12, vol 9, main work. Pencil points to cycloheptan-carbonsäure
This is the entry in the main work, and here we have the same arrangement as previously: names, followed by structure, then methods of preparation and relevant references.

S35 Same as S34, showing abbreviation of author's names
If a reference is cited again in the same entry, only the first two letters of the author's name are repeated, so that here Ei and Wi refers to Einhorn and Wilstatter, cited earlier in the entry.

S36 Page 13, vol 9, main work, showing remainder of entry. Pencil points to Farbloses
Properties are detailed on page 13 after the preparations and as you can see here, derivatives are given at the end of the entry.

S37 Page 7, vol 9, first supplement. Pencil points to ' V '
If the compound occurs naturally, this is indicated after the structure by ' V ' for ' Vorkommen ', or ' occurrence ', as shown here in the entry in the first supplement. In the supplements, the reference.

S38 Same as S37. Pencil points to S12
after the structure is to the main entry, so ' S12 ' after the structure in the first supplement indicates ' Seite ' or page 12 in the main work.

S39 Page 9, vol 9, second supplement. Pencil points to ' H12 ', ' E17 '
The second supplement used ' H12 ', H standing for Hauptwerk, and ' E17 ' standing for Erganzungswerk, to refer to earlier entries.

S40 Spine of volume of third supplement
So far you have collected information on your compound up to 1929. In order to up-date this you should consult the third supplement which is in process of publication. Until it is complete with cumulative subject and formula indexes, you need to look in

S41 Page 924, vol 9, third supplement (subject index). Pencil points to compound
the index at the end of the appropriate volume. Page 924 in volume 9 contains the index entry for ' Cycloheptan-carbonsäure '.

S42 Page 47, vol 9, third supplement, entry for cycloheptan-carbonsäure
This refers you to page 47 for the entry for this compound, seen here at the top of the page, thus bringing your information up to 1949.

S43 ' Bottle ' ' Mellon ', and ' Runquist '. Guides to using Beilstein books
on a table top

You will find an explanation of the classification system used in *Beilstein* in
guides to the literature of chemistry, such as Bottle's *Use of the chemical
literature* and Mellon's *Chemical publications*; also helpful is Runquist's
A programmed guide to Beilstein's ' Handbuch '. A detailed knowledge of
the system is not necessary for most literature searches, but occasionally you
may wish to look up the properties of a class of compounds—say the refractive
indexes of amino esters—when this knowledge would be useful.

S44 Reader consulting Beilstein at the shelves

The reasons why you will find *Beilstein* helpful are its reliability, comprehensive coverage and its collection of data from many sources. This often
makes it unnecessary to consult earlier guides to chemical literature, which
may be difficult to get hold of.

S45 Reader consulting Beilstein at a desk

As you have seen, it lists information on every known organic compound and
for each gives, in abbreviated form, its structure, configuration, occurrence,
physical, chemical and physiological properties and methods of preparation,
including the preferred method.

S46 Reader consulting Beilstein recording references

All this information is referenced, so that you are also provided with a
complete literature search for each compound.

S47 ' Chemical abstracts ' and ' Chemisches zentralblatt ' (books on a table)

By contrast, the information in *Chemical abstracts* and its German counter-
part, *Chemisches zentralblatt,* is scattered, so that finding a compound in
Beilstein, may save you hours of searching through *Chemical abstracts* and
similar publications.

S48 Open page of ' Chemical abstracts '

But remember that *Beilstein* extends only up to 1949, and is therefore no
guide to the recent literature. If you need information after this date, you
should consult *Chemical abstracts*.

*S49 ' Chemical titles ', ' Current contents ' and ' Current abstracts of chem-
istry and Index chemicus '* (books on a table top)

or for the most recent literature, current awareness journals, such as *Chemical
titles, Current contents: Physical and chemical sciences* or *Current abstracts
of chemistry and index chemicus*.

In this talk we have been able to cover only the main features and uses of *Beilstein*. We hope that it has given you the basic facts on which to build a more detailed knowledge of its uses and resources by examining the volumes for yourself.

5 FILM SCRIPT

The script of the Central Office of Information short film 'Automated library' is reproduced by permission of the Central Office of Information.

AUTOMATED LIBRARY

1   Tracking shot, Liz Ferris walking over bridge outside library.
Hello—Liz Ferris from Britain, where I'm visiting a new and rather special library. These days with the opening up of vast new areas of knowledge and the corresponding explosion of the printed word, finding your way through mazes of information can be a bit of a puzzle. In the Middle Ages it was easy—students only had one copy of a book and passed it round between them—but nowadays so *much* is written that it's often difficult to find what you really want.

2   Liz Ferris enters door and goes in. Goes up to notice board and looks at notice. Zoom into big close up of her and notice.
Here at Hatfield Polytechnic they have installed a system that makes navigating a complex reference library child's play. *Turns to notice.* It is based on colour-coded routes that lead you to your destination, and the exact piece of information you want, in no time at all.

3   Liz walks right of frame. She walks towards desk, back to camera. Camera tilts up to notice over her head. She goes to contents panel and reads.
Imagine that I'm an engineering student looking for the most recent book on, say, electric motor cars. I look up *engineering* on the panel—and I see that it's coded with a square red signal, and it's on the 2nd floor of the library. All I have to do then is follow that red square.

4   Mute montage shots of Liz following through red square on various information panels. Entrance to stairs, and entrance to department. Liz comes through doors in relevant department by information station. . . .
Well, now I've got here I can see that a *book* on electric cars doesn't exist, so I'll have to look amongst the technical abstracts to see what *is* available —I've obviously chosen a rather complicated subject. But even here, all the donkey work is done for you—by this information station.

5   Liz sits down and puts on earphones.
Voice off: On every floor in the library there is an automatic information station.

6   Cutaway to tape recorder.

It consists of prerecorded tapes that work in conjunction with a series of charts.

7   Close up charts.

8   Liz gets up and walks round library.

The tapes are transmitted by an inductive loop system which allows the student complete freedom anywhere in the room.

9   Cutaway to loop system.

I can listen to it as I move around, and nobody else in the library is disturbed by it.

10   Close up Liz by shelves.

Voice from tape recorder: Abstracts are short cuts to information . . .

11   Liz reaches required section, takes out paper and takes off headphones.

Well I've found my paper and it took me only a few minutes—and that would have been the same in any other section of the library. Most students would have needed a specialist course of tutorials to teach them how to wade through all these codes and sub-codes, especially in these days when the material is continually being updated and modified.

12   Liz Ferris outside study carrels.

Even a stranger like myself can find my way around.

13   Cutaway to green signal.

This time I'm a language student, following the green signal which denotes tapes and records.

14   Record put on by technician.

When I've selected the record, it's put on the master console, and I can retire to my private study-cubicle to listen to it.

15   Liz turns on switch. (Bring up sound of tape with language lesson.)

16   Student pushing portable carrel into position.

There are portable cubicles too at which any student can enjoy the same facilities—each one has an outlet for a slide projector and a recorder.

17   Student turns on projector. Zoom in to picture (silent shot).

18   Cutaway to microfilm store.

Of course the ultimate in space and time economy is a microfilm and microfiche store.

19   Microfilm reader.

20   Close up of screen.

The retrieval system in operation here is perhaps indicative of the way in which all information will be dealt with in the future—the library will come to you, not you to it.

21   Close up of Liz Ferris holding book.

But in the meantime the Hatfield system is the nearest we can come to total automation in storage and retrieval. As long as we're still relying on those old fashioned things called books, we want the easiest and most accurate method of using them—until the day when we all have our own personal computer.

SOME AIDS AVAILABLE FOR LOAN
OR PURCHASE

MASSACHUSETTS INSTITUTE OF TECHNOLOGY Project Intrex
Synchronised sound slide programs:

Barker Engineering Library subject catalog, $2\frac{1}{2}$ minutes synchronised sound-slide program. This is a brief introduction for the new user of the library.

Barker Engineering Library author-title catalog, $2\frac{1}{2}$ minutes synchronised sound-slide program. This was made with the same intent as the program on the subject catalog.

Engineering index
3 minutes synchronised sound-slide program.

Audio programs with sample pages:

NASA STAR
5 minutes.
Science citation index
$5\frac{1}{2}$ minutes. Some discussion.
Chemical abstracts
10 minutes.
International aerospace abstracts/NASA STAR
9 minutes.
Government reports index
7 minutes.

SCONUL (Standing Conference of National and University Libraries) at Bradford University, England, co-operative program for producing tape/slide guides to library services. Individual guides have been produced at different libraries. The following guides have been completed:
Introduction to information retrieval
(Loughborough University of Technology Library).
Guide to searching British patent literature

(National Reference Library of Science and Invention).
A basic guide to the use of Beilstein
(University of Salford Library).
Guide to the use of chemical abstracts
(University of Southampton Library).
Guide to the use of the literature in medicine and related subjects
(University of Newcastle-upon-Tyne Library).
Introduction to the literature of sociology
(Bath University of Technology Library).
Outline of the literature of chemistry
(Royal Holloway College Library).

Audio visual guide to the chemical literature
(Eastern Michigan University)
The guide is divided into 28 units; each comprises a cassetted audio tape commentary synchronised with a visual display of 2 × 2 inch colour slides. The tape recordings vary in length from one to twenty three minutes. The audio visual equipment has already been described. The general pattern of the guide is as follows:

2 units	Introduction.
13 units	Guides to chemical literature, general references, treatises, handbooks and tables.
3 units	Beilstein's *Handbuch der Organischen Chemie*.
2 units	General indexing abstracting publications.
3 units	*Chemical abstracts*.
1 unit	*Chemisches zentralblatt*.
2 units	Primary publications.
3 units	Information sources:
	Government and other sources.
	Automated search systems.
	us government publications.

Handling information. A library course for sixth forms and under-graduates (Hatfield Polytechnic, England).

The course comprises 12 cassetted tape commentaries illustrated by 105 printed charts. Recordings vary in length from 12 minutes to 20 minutes as follows:

REFERENCES

Audio visual aids mentioned in the text

FILMS

Finding information. Waterman productions released by Churchill Films, 1962, sound and colour, 11 minutes.

And something more. American Library Assn, 1964, 16 mm sound and colour, 28 minutes.

Books go walkabout. Tasmania, Dept of Film Production 1961, 16 mm sound and colour, 11 minutes.

At your request. World Wide, 1963, 16 mm sound and colour, 16 minutes.

The medlars story. National Library of Medicine, Bethesda, Maryland, 1963, 16 mm sound black and white, 24 minutes.

Library of Congress. Encyclopedia Britannica and Library of Congress, 1969, 16 mm sound, colour and black and white, 23 minutes.

SBN 72. BBC Television Enterprises, 1972, 16 mm sound black and white, 20 minutes.

TWIB Automated library. Central Office of Information, 1971, 16 mm sound black and white, 5 minutes.

Library research in high school. Kugler-Barker Productions, 1959, 16 mm sound and colour, 10 minutes.

FILM STRIPS

The card catalogue. Library Filmstrip Centre, Wichita, Kansas, 1968, 35 mm, 46 frames, colour.

Dewey decimal system (Library Series). Young American Films, New York, 1950, 35 mm, 45 frames, black and white.

Use your library: for better grades and fun too. Society for Visual Education, Chicago, 1959, 35 mm, 81 frames, black and white.

What can I find in the encyclopedia. Visual Education Consultants, Madison, 1958, 35 mm, 30 frames, black and white.

LITERATURE CITED

1 Shirley L Hopkinson: *Instructional materials for teaching the use of the library.* San Jose, California, Claremont House, 1971.

2 O Bertrand Ramsay: *An audio-visual guide to the chemical literature. Journal of chemical documentation* 9(2) May 1969, 92-95.

4

Library literature

THE GENERATION OF 'library literature' is perhaps the oldest and most widely used method of exploiting resources in all types of library. The quantity of this material is enormous and it is extremely varied in presentation and format. The term 'library literature' includes all those printed or mimeographed 'house' publications with which most librarians are familiar. The term includes book lists, rules and opening time cards; introductions to the library, with notes on the catalogue; the detailed guides to library stock and services; and, the comprehensive guides to subject fields which are produced by academic libraries.

The main purpose of this chapter is to show how this printed material extends and co-ordinates the effect of the visual and audio-visual elements in an exploitation system. It will, however, be helpful to discuss some of the factors which have to be considered when preparing this material.

The first consideration must always be to decide exactly what the librarian wishes to achieve from the publication. It is as well to remember, too, that unless a library user reads a hand-out, it has no purpose, whether it is a list of 'books for gardeners' issued by a branch public library or a comprehensive search tool for graduate students in a university. Next, it is necessary to decide the kind of readers the literature is designed to inform or instruct. The third decision will be concerned with the amount of detail and how much information should be included in a proposed publication. As a general rule, it is suggested that the ideal is that any library publication should contain the minimum amount of detail which will achieve the purpose for which it is designed.

Finally, it is necessary to decide on the physical layout: the size of page, number of pages, size of print; and the illustrations which will be included. It will also be important to decide whether colour will be used in the text or the illustrations.

In any library the purposes of library literature lie under five main heads:

1 To establish the library's prestige and to develop good public relations. Typical examples of this type of publication are the various items commemorating the opening of a new library. However, this aspect of the library's relationship with its readers is also expressed through the general quality and appearance of all its library literature.

A somewhat unusual example of this public relations information is an attractively illustrated booklet distributed to readers of Birmingham Central Library, England, on the occasion of moving to new premises. The timetable for the move is shown graphically by means of a block diagram of the library with the sections of it indicated by hatchings of various density to correspond to the transfer period. Each stage of the move is carefully explained for the readers, so that they may suffer as little inconvenience as possible during the period of moving. For the librarians there is a bibliography of fourteen journal articles, describing major library moves, which, in the last ten years, have taken place in Australia, New Zealand, the United States of America and Britain.

2 To make readers aware of the library's administrative detail as it affects the library user, for example, hours of opening, borrowing arrangements, interloan facilities, fines for overdue loans, conditions for readers (silent areas, smoking areas, areas reserved for library staff, etc).

3 To give news of the new developments and the changes in library administration which affect readers, and to give information about additions to the library's resources: new books, new services, and new staff.

4 To supply information which makes the reader aware of the various books and services which the library has to offer. This information comes in very many forms, varying from single sheet hand-outs to comprehensive literature guides.

5 To give instruction. This type of publication includes all the literature given or sold to readers so that they may learn how to use the library facilities more easily.

Individual items of library literature will usually serve something of all these purposes. In physical form, this material falls into three general categories.

1 Single-idea publications, usually on slips of paper or cards and made widely available to readers of all kinds. Examples are public library reading lists, (' Books for fishermen '), library opening times, branches and addresses, etc. One polytechnic library has issued a series of bookmarks, entitled, ' *You study . . . useful class numbers to remember* '. The cards are issued for twenty five subject areas. On each card is listed a couple of dozen topics within the subject area, showing the relevant classification numbers used.

2 Single page or short guides designed to present to readers a broad view of the services offered by the library. These hand-outs come from all types of library, and frequently include floor plans, notes on reference books, and directions for using the catalogue, as well as the notes on administrative detail such as the library rules, hours of opening and borrowing procedures.

3 Booklets of various sizes serving three broad purposes:

(i) To give the borrower a more detailed picture of the books and services offered by the library, that is to say, to cover the ground in the single-sheet guide but in much greater detail. For example, the contents of a small college library guide contained the following sections:

(*a*) Library hours—loans of books and periodicals—renewals of loans—enquiries—library rules.

(*b*) Historical note.

(*c*) Classification and cataloguing: Universal Decimal Classification, its form and purpose—Author/title catalogue—subject or classified catalogue—subject index.

(*d*) Using the catalogue—finding books, pamphlets, periodicals—information recorded in the catalogue.

(*e*) Documents in the college library: books—reference books—periodicals—pamphlets—report series—standards—patents—abstracting publications—bibliographies—maps, atlases—commercial information—careers.

(*f*) Other library services: loans from other libraries—micro-texts—photocopying—drawing board—translations—study rooms.

(*g*) Getting the best from your library. Hints on finding and using information.

(ii) Comprehensive guides to the literature of a subject. This type of publication has until recently come from the libraries of teaching institutions, but public libraries now have an increasingly important part to play in supplying books for students, especially those studying at the universities in the large cities of Britain and the USA. Public libraries also frequently cater for the needs of industry, which requires similar comprehensive information.

These guides are most commonly prepared for students taking a course of study, part of the requirement for which is a thesis, project report or term essay. The purpose of the guide is to outline a programme which can be followed when undertaking a literature search on a specific subject in a particular library. The content and presentation of these guides depends upon the type of student and his or her academic training; on the kind of library and its facilities, including, to some extent, the other library facilities in the nearby area; and, lastly, on the subject field. For example, a search in a historical subject follows a different pattern from that for a search in the literature of chemistry. In general, these literature guides cover the following topics:

(*a*) An introduction to search techniques.

(*b*) Notes on the organisation of the library: the library classification, how to use the catalogue and find books in the shelves, borrowing conditions and services available (inter-loan arrangements, microfilm readers, photocopying facilities).

(*c*) Suitable general reference sources, dictionaries, encyclopedias, directories, etc.

(*d*) Suitable reference sources for special subject areas (bibliographies, treatises, handbooks, standard texts).

(*e*) Bibliographic aids (periodicals, indexes, abstracting publications, review series, and current awareness sources).

(*f*) Special areas of information: government and state publications, learned and professional society publications, organisations for research, patent specifications, Standard specifications.

(*g*) Notes on other libraries in the area which have useful collections or offer special services.

Frequently the notes on search techniques are followed by instructions for presenting information in the form of an essay or a report. All but the shortest of these guides include a detailed list of contents, and some have an index.

(iii) A third group of multi-page publications which also relate to teaching or special libraries comprises *accessions lists* (new additions to library stock). These lists are usually arranged in a subject order and sometimes include brief annotations. In some libraries such lists are issued at frequent intervals as a current awareness service for readers. A somewhat similar purpose is served by the various lists of special publications held in the library. The most widely available of such lists record the periodicals received by the library. Such periodicals lists are also useful to other libraries, since information about local periodical collections can speed up the interloan processes. For readers, such lists can be particularly valuable, when using bibliographical aids, as a check on the availability of references, but there is some further discussion of this topic later in this chapter.

(iv) Finally, each individual library is part of a wider library service. The interchange of ideas between librarians is of direct importance to the profession as a whole. It is therefore frequently worth while to have a visitors guide aimed at the needs of librarians. Such people, who are not prospective users of the library, are interested in the library buildings, the furniture, and the equipment, in the library organisation, in the details of experimental techniques and in new materials and devices. Layout plans, photographs of equipment and specifications of materials are likely to be important in such printed matter.

METHODS OF PRODUCTION OF LIBRARY LITERATURE

Having decided upon the purpose of the publication and the

amount of information which it will contain, the next step will be to consider what the completed publication will look like. Normally, there are four methods of production:

1 Preparation by typewriter with some form of mimeograph reproduction.

2 Typescript with photocopy reproduction.

3 Making a paper or metal plate from a typescript master and reproduction by offset printer.

4 Reproduction by a commercial printing firm.

The two limiting factors are always the amount of money the librarian has to spend and the facilities for reproduction which are available to him. Apart from these limitations, the two most important considerations are the number of copies required, and how long the information in the proposed publication is likely to be useful. Remembering, in the words of Ranganathan, that a library is a ' growing organism ', the information in library literature is never static. However, reading lists, with other single sheet hand-outs and the regular lists of accessions may be regarded as having a much shorter period of usefulness than would be so for a detailed library guide to the literature of a subject or, say, a complete list of the periodicals received by a library.

When a comparatively few copies are required of a one- or two-page publication, stencil duplicating will be the cheapest form of reproduction. Library literature in this form is readable and line drawings can be reproduced reasonably well. The quality is adequate for ephemeral hand-out information. As an alternative, photocopying, especially electrostatic or ' dry copying ', usually gives reproductions of better quality. A much wider range of materials can be used to produce the ' masters ' from which copies are to be made. A master in this context refers to the original materials which are to be copied. Usually this is mainly typescript, but sample pages with extracts from printed papers of various kinds can be copied, and the layout of a master can include hand lettering, typescript or transfer lettering such as *Letraset*. For a few copies the cost of reproduction by this means compares with that for stencil duplicating. If a large number of copies of a library publication is required, very good quality printing may be achieved by making offset printing plates on an electrostatic or dry copier. Such plates are made either of prepared paper or of thin metal. Paper plates are suitable when a few hundred copies are required. Metal plates are used when some thousands of copies are needed. The masters may contain the same material as for the paper copies which are described above. Best results are obtained from black and white masters, but some colours may be used for making a master. Although paper copies made on a dry copier can only be produced in black and white, when the plates are used on an offset printer, it is possible to print in more than one colour, although extra colours add considerably to the cost of production. Where more than, say, 200 copies of a library publication are required, offset printing in this way is the most economical form of reproduction.

None of the reproduction methods mentioned so far can print half-tone photographs really well, and where high quality printing is required, the work will be done most satisfactorily by a commercial printer.

The above few notes are but the briefest outline of the three commonest methods of full size document copying. For a detailed treatment of this topic there are two useful books, by S B Page[1], and B Mason[2].

Before going on to discuss the place of library literature in a system of guiding, it may be helpful to mention the increasingly large number of commercially published guides to subject literature. Although these *subject guides* are not generally written with a particular library in mind, they can be very valuable as an aid to the exploitation of the resources in any library. For example, a librarian whose particular interest is history and English literature may be required to deal with somebody wanting information in chemistry. In such an event, if a copy of Bottle's guide to chemical literature is to hand, the combination of the librarian's understanding of the pattern of library organisation, the chemist's knowledge of his subject and a good guide to the literature of chemistry is likely to produce reasonably useful results. These guides vary a great deal in content and organisation. Some are based upon lecture notes for students in colleges or universities. Bottle's book, mentioned above, was originally based upon a series of papers read at a seminar, although the original text has now been revised several times. Some of the guides are mainly an annotated bibliography. However, in general, each guide will make some analysis of the structure of the subject field and of the literature in it. The text will include the major reference sources, the bibliographic aids which will be useful and, usually, notes on the more important periodical literature. For example, the changes in titles and in the method of numbering volumes. Some guides are very long and exhaustive and are written for specialists and for people doing research. Others are short and selective, written for students and librarians in small libraries. At the end of this chapter is a short list of some of these guides.

OUTLINES OF GUIDES FROM WORKING LIBRARIES

Finsbury Library Service, England.

A handbook for teachers. 20 pp, multi-coloured. The booklet contains the following sections: books for work and recreation, visual aids, gramophone records, children's lending library, school libraries, class visits to the library, book guidance, homework, special activities, school holidays, good readers' club, backward readers, visits to schools (by librarians on the staff of the library).

Free Library of Philadelphia, USA.

How to use the library: a guide for students in high school and junior college. 24 p, black and white. Sections include: how books are arranged: Dewey main classes with examples of annotated catalogue cards; reference books: encyclopedias, yearbooks, dictionaries, facts about people, indexes to magazines and newspapers, indexes to parts of books, additional material on authors and their works. For each section there is a list of titles with short annotations. In the last pages the reader is told about the various departments of the central library and reminded how to search for a book. Finally, there are two pages of notes on how to attack an assignment. There is then a list of the library's branches and two blank pages for notes.

University of Strathclyde, Scotland.
Library guide. 14 p. This is a very short guide in six sections with a thumb index: introduction—general information; borrowing and library regulations—using the catalogue; library floor plans; serials publications—facilities and services; the Andersonian library: a brief historical sketch; some major bibliographical aids and references grouped under subjects.

Colorado State University Libraries, USA.
Library handbook for faculty and graduate students. 20 p, two colours. There are six main sections: general information; collections of the library, which deals with book recommendations and purchases; locating information—how to use the catalogue, annotated catalogue cards (colour used for emphasis), also a two colour block drawing of a library premises on four floors with a numbered key to the books and services available; services for readers —loans, interlibrary loan, photo-duplication, Medlars searches, reserving items for students' reserved book collections; special services—instructions for use of the library resources (including a 45-minute videotape lecture), seminar rooms, staff lounge shared by library staff and faculty members; library locator, an A-Z guide to finding library books and facilities.

University of Aston in Birmingham, England.
Readers guide to chemistry and chemical engineering. 12 p, black and white. Arranged under broad subject headings: general guides, guides to scientific literature, guides to the literature of chemistry and chemical engineering and related subjects, general guides to periodicals, guides to chemistry and chemical engineering periodicals, current awareness publications, guide to abstracts, general abstracts (titles), abstracts dealing with chemistry and applied chemistry, specialised abstracts, abstracts (sections) in journals, review series, translations, theses, patents, standards. Each section includes a list of titles with brief annotations.

LIBRARY LITERATURE IN A SYSTEM FOR EXPLOITING LIBRARY RESOURCES

In the last two chapters we have discussed the first three elements in an exploitation program. Permanent visual information, colour coded guiding and some of the audio-visual devices which can be used to amplify the instruction provided by labels and printed instruction panels.

In this chapter we have examined some of the examples of library literature issued by working libraries. We also considered the general purposes served by library literature: to promote good public relations, to make readers aware of library facilities and to instruct them in the use of the library and the information in it. For the librarian these guides are a valuable reference source when giving readers personal advice. In looking at the individual examples of printed guides, it will be noticed that a good deal of effort is expended on telling people where the books and services are to be found. The commonest way of giving this information is by means of floor plans. The Colorado State University library guide included a block diagram with a numbered location index in the centre of the guide, while at the back there was a detailed index of library facilities and services, showing the location of each. It will be noticed, too, that printed guides are reference sources to which less detailed or less permanent forms of instruction can be referred. For example, the University of Illinois' film ' Your library ' continually referred the viewer back to the printed guide of the same title.

In a library resources exploitation program, the purpose of the printed guides and other library literature is to co-ordinate the various elements in the guiding program; to extend and amplify information received from signs and labels of various kinds; to increase the usefulness of instruction at *information stations*; and to provide information which is valuable because it is portable. Finally, the library's printed guides provide an alternative way for readers to learn how to use the library. Some people prefer to take in information by reading. A further important function performed by the specific guides in a library exploitation program is to provide a textbook for any comprehensive library instruction classes.

As in the other elements of the exploitation scheme, the printed guides are designed to answer the reader's three basic questions : what has the library to offer to its readers; where are the facilities to be found; and, when found, how can they be used effectively with a minimum waste of time. Once again, although primarily designed to serve readers, the printed guides are a valuable means of saving time for library staff. As has been noted in the examples quoted, the content of printed guides will depend upon the organisation of the library and the type of reader which the library serves. In general, it is suggested that there should be a brief general guide and one or more specific guides.

In considering any kind of library, it must be borne in mind that a large proportion of the information in printed guides and similar publications will not be read; and much of what is read will not be significant to the reader at the time of reading. That is to say, the information will not relate to an immediate need. Probably the shorter the message the more likely it is to be received. Diagrammatic information may have a greater impact than the text, and bold headings help to accentuate the structure of information. Comparatively few library users, even in academic libraries, make literature searches in depth, and therefore the average reader does not have a strong motive for reading detailed or specific information about the library's resources. With suitable advice from library staff, however, many more readers will find useful information in detailed guides. For this reason, wide free distribution of specific guides is a wasteful practice. There may be, in fact, an argument in favour of making a small charge to readers for any detailed instructive literature. It is a weakness of human nature that the things which are free are usually regarded as being less valuable than those which have to be paid for. Nevertheless, copies of these guides should be widely available for reference by readers in the library.

The purpose of a general printed guide in a guiding plan is, first, to make readers aware of the organisation of the library, which includes an explanation of the various elements of the exploitation scheme; secondly, to inform them of the books and services the library has to offer; and, lastly, to set out the conditions of library use, hours of opening and loan procedure. The specific guides are designed to aid people wishing to use the library in some depth. Their purpose is to give in greater detail the information and instruction provided by the signs and labels and by the other visual and audio aids in the guiding scheme. It may be helpful at this point to examine, in brief detail, the printed guides used in a working library system.

PRINTED GUIDES IN THE EXPLOITATION PROGRAM OF A WORKING LIBRARY

This example is from a polytechnic library in England. The elements in the library resources exploitation program include the following:

Visual and audio aids

  1 Introductory film, 'Automated library', of five minutes duration and described in chaper 3.

  2 Information and instruction labels and panels with colour coded hanging signs as described in chapter 2.

  3 Information stations, pre-recorded instruction illustrated by printed charts, transmitted through reader operated tape recorders as described in chapter 3, as follows:

    (i) Using the Universal Decimal Classification and the library catalogue.

    (ii) Using indexing/abstracting publications in the humanities.

    (iii) Using indexing/abstracting publications in technology.

    (iv) Using *Chemical abstracts.*

Printed guides

  1 *A brief library guide*—1 page.

  2 *A guide to the use of periodicals and report series*—30 pages.

  3 *How to find out,* a guide to the use of the catalogue, bibliographies, abstracts, reviews—26 pages.

  4 *Where to find out.* Government publications, research organisations, patents, standards—20 pages.

1 *A brief library guide.* This is a single sheet of A4 paper folded to make four pages. The information includes the following details:

Subject departments in the library. The subject information is set out diagrammatically as in the main contents panel which readers can see at the entrance to the library and on each stair landing.

Notes on the organisation of information in the library: three subject floors and a main service floor; subject division is based upon Universal Decimal Classification. Finding the information you need: colour coded guiding designed to lead the reader to the required books or services.

Services: catalogue; interloan; photocopying; microtext readers; gramophone records and tape recordings; information stations; borrowing books; reserved textbook collection; library hours; thinking of others.

This guide is printed from typescript under headings with very brief details. Its purpose is to introduce readers to the subject divisions of the library and the self service facilities. This leaflet is widely distributed and is particularly useful for readers making a brief tour of the library. It is also a useful reference source for people after seeing the film 'Automated library'.

2 *A guide to the use of periodicals and report series.* This is a detailed guide in two sections as indicated by the title. Each section of the guide includes introductory notes and a list of periodicals and report series held in the library. Details of the contents headings of this guide are:

(i) PERIODICALS: *Introductory notes and definitions, Languages, Problems in using periodical references, Some reference sources which can aid in solving these problems, Using this periodicals list, Periodicals from other libraries, Abbreviations used in this list.* Then follows a list of periodicals held in the library.

(ii) REPORT SERIES: *Introductory notes and definitions, Reports (classified, unclassified), Numbering of report series, Problems in following up references to report series, Some helpful aids, Avail-ability of report series, Using this list.* Then follows a list of report series received by the library.

This guide serves several purposes. In library instruction, it is a textbook for the study of periodical literature, which provides standard definitions for terms used and draws attention to periodicals in foreign languages and the facilities for translation. It also summarises the problems readers are likely to face when following up periodical references, and records the biblio-graphic aids which may be useful in solving some of these diffi-culties.

For library staff from whom readers are seeking advice, the introductory notes are a ready source of reference where informa-tion can be pin-pointed for a reader. Verbal advice supported by printed information is likely to be more easily understood, and will save time for both the reader and the librarian. The *list of periodicals* is, perhaps, most useful for a reader who is making a search through the indexing and abstracting publications. During such a search it is always useful to know which references are available in the search library. This list can be consulted at any place in the library where the abstracts are shelved. For this reason it is important that the list of library holdings should include the dates of the volumes held and the shelf location of each title.

The *report literature list* is used somewhat differently. Al-though individual reports are covered by the relevant abstracting services, it is often useful for a searcher in a subject area to browse through a file of reports issued by an organisation known to be carrying out research in the subject field. For example, an engineer in Britain, especially one interested in automatic control of machines, would probably find useful information in several of the reports issued by the National Engineering Laboratory. Also, such organisations publish from time to time lists of all the reports which have been issued. By listing these reports series in this guide, readers become aware of the series which are immediately available in the library. Similarly this information can also act as a reminder to library staff.

1A: *Simple, clear labelling at Cathkin Branch Library, Lanark County, Scotland.*

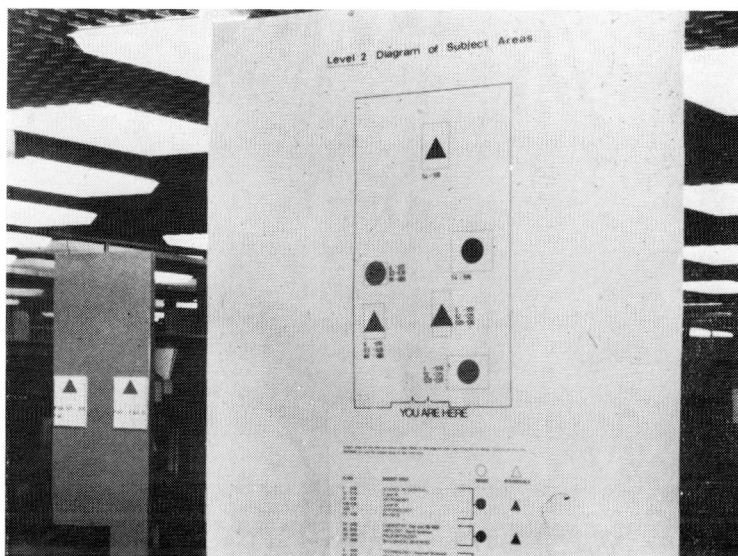

1B: *Contents panel and colour coded guiding at T L Robertson Library, Western Australian Institute of Technology, Bentley, WA.*

2A: *Stack-end information in a special library in England.*

2B: *Shelf guiding and contents panels at Ralston Branch Library, Renfrew County, Scotland.*

3A: *Colour coded visual information at the Hatfield Polytechnic Library, England. Note the catalogue information station.*

3B: *Contents information and stack labels at the Central Library, Newcastle-upon-Tyne, England.*

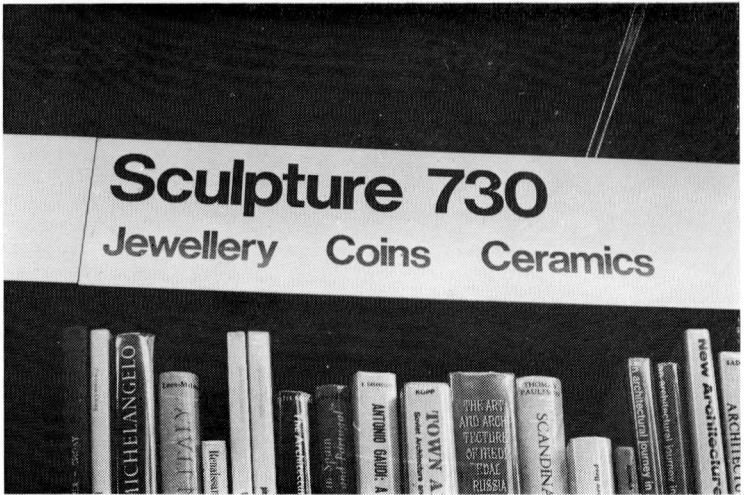

4A: *Moveable book stack guides at South Norwood Branch, Lambeth Public Libraries, London, England.*

4B: *Detailed labelling at Monroe County Public Library, Indiana, USA.*

5:

MATERIALS AND FITTINGS FOR SETTING UP A COLOUR CODED GUIDING PROGRAM:

Printing surface material is white paper bonded to straw board. Contents information panels (nos 3, 6, 12) were prepared photographically from typed masters. Coloured signals were applied to all signs by using squares or circles of gummed coloured paper. Captions (nos 1, 2, 4, 7, 9, 11) were hand-lettered with a fibre tipped pen and all printing surfaces were protected with transpaseal film.

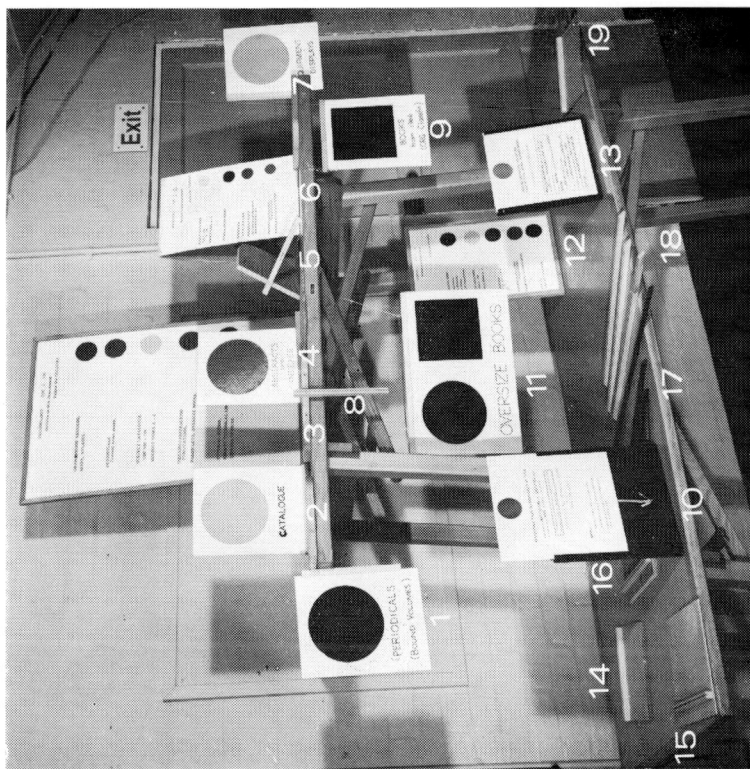

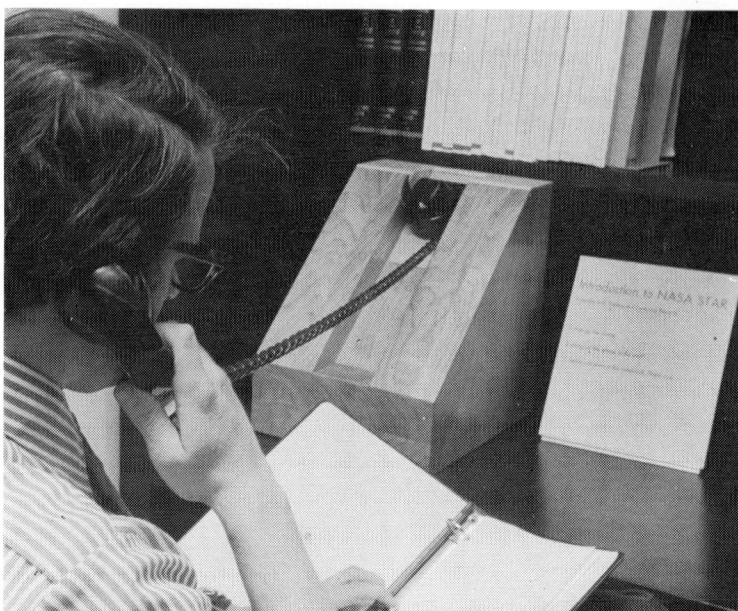

6A: *A reader using an audio guide in the Barker Engineering Library, Massachusetts Institute of Technology, Cambridge, USA.*

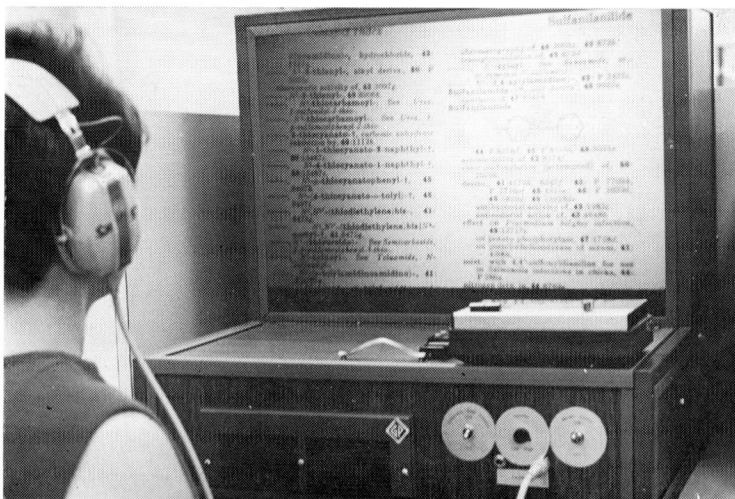

6B: *A student receives instruction in the use of* Chemical abstracts *at the audio-graph console at Eastern Michigan University, USA.*

7A: *A reader listens in to a tape/slide instruction program on the console designed at Surrey University, England.*

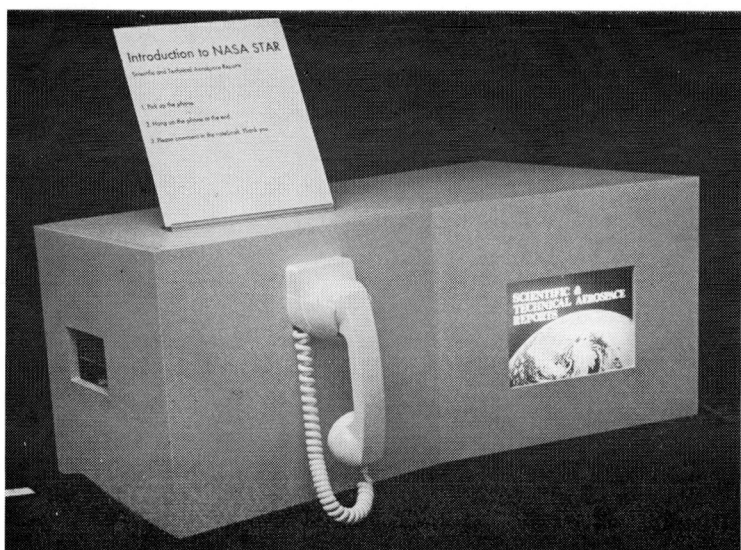

7B: *The sound slide unit introducing* NASA *STAR in the Barker Engineering Library at Massachusetts Institute of Technology, Cambridge, USA.*

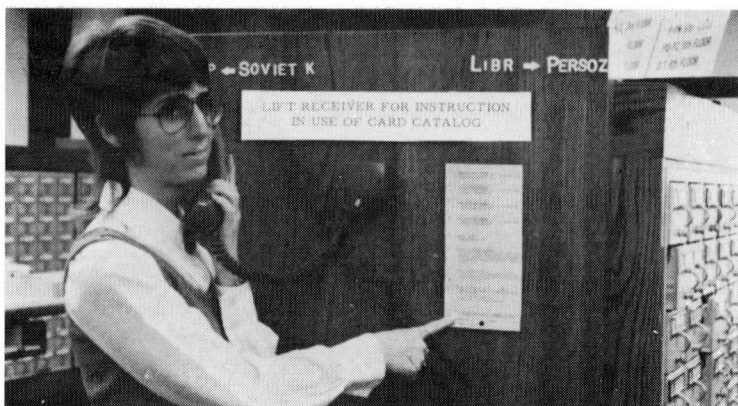

8A: *Receiving instruction in catalogue use at Hofstra University, New York, USA.*

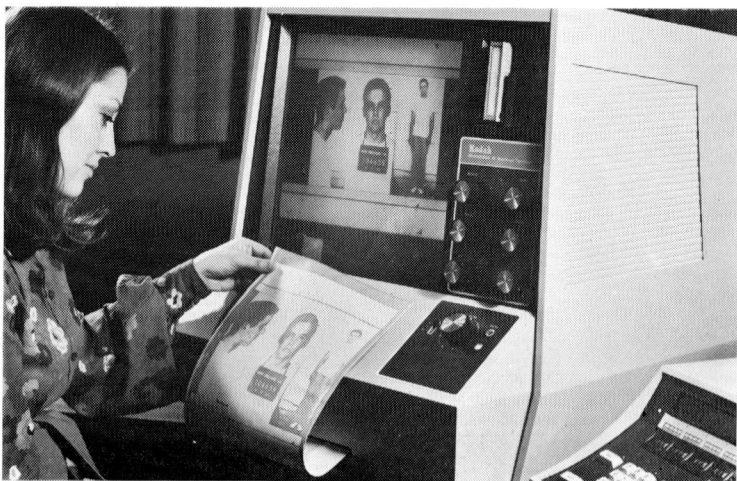

8B: *Kodak Miracode microfilm reader with printout facility. (Photo by courtesy of manufacturers.)*

3 *How to find out, a guide to the use of the catalogue, biblio-graphies, abstracts, reviews.* This is a guide in four sections which is designed as an aid to people wishing to use these library facilities. There are brief instructions for use at the beginning of each section, which are followed by a list of relevant titles held in the library. Details of the contents of the guide are as follows:

(i) THE UNIVERSAL DECIMAL CLASSIFICATION, USING THE LIBRARY CATALOGUE: *Purposes, principles, examples.*

(ii) GENERAL BIBLIOGRAPHIES: *Definitions, (. . .) Bibliography, General bibliography, Coverage of information, In print, Out of print, Information supplied, Likely use for general bibliographies.*

(iii) INDEXING AND ABSTRACTING PUBLICATIONS: *Definitions. Indexing publications, contents, Abstracting publications, contents, Some problems in using indexing/abstracting publications.*

(iv) REVIEWS OF PROGRESS: *Definition, Review coverage, Publication.*

Again this guide serves several purposes. For library instruction classes, it forms a reference text for instruction in the use of the catalogue and the Universal Decimal Classification, and for instruction in using the various bibliographic aids. The information in each section of the guide can also be used in a similar way by members of the library staff who need to give advice to individual readers. By listing the titles of *Abstracts* and *Review series,* students in library classes are made aware of the wide range of these publications, while the index at the back of the guide helps to gather together reviews and abstracts for people with a particular subject interest. Finally, when using the *abstracts information stations,* the reader is referred back to the guide as a reference text as a means of extending and amplifying the audio instruction.

4 *Where to find out.* Government publications, research organisations, patents, standards. This guide is in four sections and provides for another approach to finding information in a search program. Such a program can be considered in four stages; a broad search using dictionaries, encyclopedias and similar quick reference books; a more specific reading of books and pamphlets,

found through the catalogue; the gathering of references by the use of bibliographic aids; and, lastly, a search of specific areas of information. This guide caters for some of the more important of these specific areas. Topics covered by the four sections include the following:

(i) BRITISH GOVERNMENT PUBLICATIONS: *Parliamentary papers, Non parliamentary papers, Aids to finding government publications, Finding government publications in the library, References.*

(ii) RESEARCH AND DEVELOPMENT ORGANISATIONS: *Definition, Areas of research in Britain, Central government research, Research in private industry, Sponsored research, Publication of research results, Examining a typical organisation, Aids to finding information about research in Britain.*

(iii) PATENTS: *Steps in taking out a patent, Official journal (patents), Information in a patent specification, Obtaining a patent specification.*

(iv) STANDARDS: *Definition, British Standards Institution, Stages in issuing a British Standard, Information in a British Standard, Finding British Standards specifications in the library, References.*

This guide is rather more of a reference text than a bibliography. Its purpose is to explain certain patterns of publication, and to encourage a wider use of these areas of information, especially the publications by the central government. The effectiveness of this guide in exploiting library resources depends upon the way that this information is introduced to readers, whether in a library class or through personal contact with library staff.

NEWS AND SHORT TERM INFORMATION

In any library, the conditions—that is, the book stocks, the library services and the library staff are constantly changing, and it is part of any exploitation program to keep readers in touch with the developments likely to affect the relationship between the library and its readers. This kind of information is useful only over short periods, and it will be more effective if it is transmitted first in broad outline on a *notice or news board* which is placed at the entrance to the library, or at some other place where all the people coming to the library will see it.

Brief mention has already been made of this *news board* and the printed leaflets which follow up the information put on it. In the particular exploitation scheme which we have been discussing, these *information leaflets* are issued as a uniform numbered series on yellow paper. Some examples of topics dealt with in this way were: the announcement of the establishment of a tape/chart facility in the library; the changes in borrowing procedure; and, the notice of a proposed library survey for which cooperation from readers was requested. In general the information on the notice board was very brief and in lettering large enough to be read from anywhere in the service area. Each such message ended, ' Please ask at the counter for detailed leaflet '.

REFERENCES

1 S B Page: *Modern office copying*. Deutsch, 1966.

2 B Mason: *Document reproduction in libraries*. London, Assn of Assistant Librarians, 1968.

A SELECTION OF PUBLISHED GUIDES

GENERAL

Publications of governments

G Chandler: *How to find out*. Pergamon, 2nd ed 1966.

J L Andriot: *Guide to US government serials and periodicals*. McLean, Va, Document Index, 2nd ed 1972, 3 vols.

E Jackson: *Subject guide to major United States publications*. Chicago: American Lib Assn, 1968.

J G Ollé: *An introduction to British government publications*. London, Assn of Assistant Librarians, 2nd ed 1972.

J E Pemberton: *British official publications*. Pergamon, 1971.

L F Schmeckebier and R B Eastin: *Government publications and their use*. Brookings Institution, 2nd ed 1969.

US Library of Congress: *Monthly check list of state publications*.

Philosophy, psychology

D H Borchardt: *How to find out in philosophy and psychology.* Pergamon, 1968.

C K Elliott: *A guide to the documentation of psychology.* Bingley, 1971.

Social sciences, education

P R Lewis: *The literature of the social sciences: an introductory survey and guide.* London, Library Assn, 1960.

C M Waite: *Sources of information in the social sciences.* Totowa, NJ, Bedminster Press, 1964.

G A Burrington: *How to find out about statistics.* Pergamon, 1972.

J M Harvey: *Sources of statistics.* Bingley, 2nd ed 1971.

A Maltby: *Economics and commerce: the sources of information.* Bingley, 1968.

S A J Parsons: *How to find out about economics.* Pergamon, 1972.

W H Snape: *How to find out about local government.* Pergamon, 1969.

A J & M A Burke: *Documentation in education.* NY, Teachers College Press, 1967.

D J Foskett: *How to find out in educational research.* Pergamon, 1965.

Mathematics, computers, physics

N G Parke: *Guide to the literature of mathematics and physics.* Constable, 2nd ed 1959; NY, Dover, 1958.

J E Pemberton: *How to find out in mathematics.* Pergamon, 2nd ed 1969.

A Pritchard: *A guide to computer literature.* Bingley, 1972.

R H Whitford: *Physics literature: a reference manual.* Scarecrow, 1954.

B Yates: *How to find out about physics.* Pergamon, 1965.

Chemistry and geology

American Chemical Society: *Searching the chemical literature.*

The Society, 1961. Advances in chemistry series no 30.

R T Bottle: *Use of the chemical literature*. Butterworth, 2nd ed 1962.

C R Burman: *How to find out in chemistry*. Pergamon, 1965.

E J Crane, A M Patterson, E B Marr: *A guide to the literature of chemistry*. Wiley, 1957.

G M Dyson: *A short guide to chemical literature*. Longmans Green, 1951.

J Ferguson: *Bibliotheca chemica*. Verschoyle, 1954.

M G Mellon: *Chemical publications, their nature and use*. NY, McGraw-Hill, 4th ed 1965.

B Mason: *The literature of geology*. NY, The Author (American Museum of Natural History), 1953.

D C Ward and M W Wheeler: *Geologic reference sources. A subject and regional bibliography of publications and maps in the geological sciences*. Scarecrow Press, 1972.

Biological sciences

R T Bottle and H V Wyatt: *The use of biological literature*. Butterworth, 1966.

A E Kerker and E M Schlundt: *Literature sources in biological sciences*. Purdue Univ Libraries, 1961.

R C Smith: *Guide to the literature of the zoological sciences*. Burgess Publishing Co, 6th ed 1962.

A K Mukherjee: *Annotated guide to reference materials in the human sciences*. London, Asia Publishing House, 1962.

Business and industry

E T Coman: *Sources of business information*. Berkely, Los Angeles, California University Press, 2nd ed 1964; Cambridge University Press 1965.

N Burgess: *How to find out about secretarial and office practice*. Pergamon, 1967.

K G B Bakewell: *How to find out: Management and productivity*. Pergamon, 2nd ed 1970.

D Davinson: *Commercial information: a source handbook*. Pergamon, 1965.

N D Frank: *Market analysis: a handbook of current data sources*. Scarecrow Press, 1964.

N Burgess: *How to find out about banking and investment.* Pergamon, 1969.

N Burgess: *How to find out about exporting.* Pergamon, 1970.

R Brown and G A Campbell: *How to find out about the chemical industry.* Pergamon, 1969.

B Yates: *How to find out about the UK cotton industry.* Pergamon, 1967.

Applied science, medicine, engineering

D Grogan: *Science and technology: an introduction to the literature.* Bingley, 2nd 1973.

R J P Carey: *Finding and using technical information.* Edward Arnold, 1966.

F Newby: *How to find out about patents.* Pergamon, 1967.

B Houghton: *Technical information sources: a guide to patent specifications, standards and technical reports literature.* Bingley, 2nd ed 1972.

L T Morton: *How to use a medical library.* Heinemann, 4th ed 1964.

Medical Library Assn: *Handbook of medical library practice with a bibliography of the reference works and histories in medicine and the allied sciences.* Chicago, American Library Assoc, 2nd ed 1956; 3rd ed in preparation.

A L Brunn: *How to find out in pharmacy.* Pergamon, 1969.

S A J Parsons: *How to find out about engineering.* Pergamon, 1972.

B Houghton: *Mechanical engineering: the sources of information.* Bingley, 1970.

J Burkett and P Plumb: *How to find out in electrical engineering.* Pergamon, 1967.

E W Tapia: *Guide to metallurgical information.* NY, Special Libraries Assoc 1961 (SLA bibliography no 3).

D White: *How to find out in iron and steel.* Pergamon, 1970).

E R Yescombe: *Sources of information on the rubber plastics and allied industries.* Pergamon, 1968.

Art, music, architecture, planning

M W Chamberlain: *Guide to art reference books*. Chicago, American Library Assoc, 1959.

V H Duckles: *Music reference and research materials: an annotated bibliography*. London, NY, Free Press, 1964.

E T Bryant: *Music*. Bingley, 1965.

D L Smith: *How to find out in architecture and building*. Pergamon, 1967.

B White: *Sourcebook of planning information*. Bingley, 1971.

Literature

G Chandler: *How to find out about literature*. Pergamon, 1968.

A Ellis: *How to find out about children's literature*. Pergamon, 1968.

J Bate: *How to find out about Shakespeare*. Pergamon, 1968.

Geography

C S Minto: *How to find out in geography*. Pergamon, 1966.

C B M Lock: *Geography: a reference handbook*. Bingley, 2nd ed 1972.

E G Cox: *A reference guide to the literature of travel*. University of Washington, 1935-1949.

J E Pemberton: *How to find out about France*. Pergamon, 1966.

F S Stych: *How to find out about Italy*. Pergamon, 1970.

H C Campbell: *How to find out about Canada*. Pergamon, 1967.

History

P Hepworth: *How to find out in history*. Pergamon, 1966.

British Historical Association: *Help for students of history*. SPCK, 1950-, a series of booklets.

Harvard guide to American history, ed O Handlin. Harvard Univ Press, 1954.

American Historical Association: *Guide to historical literature*. NY, Macmillan, 1961.

L J Paeton: *A guide to the study of medieval history*. London, Kegan Paul, 1931; NY, Kraus, 1964. New ed in preparation.

L Madden: *How to find out about the Victorian period*. Pergamon, 1970.

5

Making self-service work

WE HAVE NOW EXAMINED the part played by the various elements in a scheme for exploiting the resources of a library: labels and signs, pre-recorded instruction and library publicity and publications.

Only a passing reference has so far been made to the importance of personal contact between the reader and the library staff. While some emphasis has been placed upon the need for self-service techniques in a library, personal service and advice to readers is an essential part of any library exploitation program. Lastly, the effectiveness of self-service aids depends upon the confidence with which people use them. Consequently, a central requirement is that such information should always be reliable and that all mechanical aids should be kept in good working order. Such a program calls for carefully supervised maintenance routines and the regular updating of information. However, before discussing how personal contact fits in to the general scheme and some of the updating techniques, it may be helpful to summarise the objectives of the exploitation program.

The following aims are common to nearly all libraries.

1 The scheme is designed to inform readers of the books and services which the library can offer; and to explain the conditions for using these facilities: which of them may be enjoyed only in the library; how many books etc may be borrowed at one time and for how long; what penalties will be incurred if books are kept longer than the permitted period, and how special arrangements are made for lending particular categories of publications, for example, reserved textbooks or periodicals.

2 It is the purpose of the scheme to make the information in the library and its services as easily accessible to readers as possible;

to do this by recording where the books etc are kept and instructing readers how to find them; and, by giving instruction in the use of books and facilities when readers are likely to be unfamiliar with them.

3 A third purpose is to give readers some understanding of the pattern behind the organisation of the library. The larger the library, the more important this aspect of exploitation becomes. It is reasonable to inform readers not only how a particular library is organised, but also why this arrangement is considered to be the most convenient one for its readers.

4 In all but the smallest library an important part of any scheme is to explain the use of the various aids to finding information. The most important of these aids is, of course, the library catalogue and the library classification scheme. As always, the types of aid to be found in individual libraries will depend upon the needs of its readers and the kind of library. In some libraries, for example a school library, readers may need instruction in the use of dictionaries and encyclopedias. In a college library, there would be a greater need to give instruction in the use of abstracts and indexing publications.

5 It is a further purpose of any exploitation scheme to extend the library experience of its readers by giving them a wider view of the library and information facilities, and by making them aware of information sources with which they have not previously come into contact.

6 Another important function of this program is to encourage a wider use of libraries and information by involving library activity with the special interests of the reader. This may be regarded as predominantly a public relations exercise, but includes an educational ingredient.

7 A more specific aspect of exploitation is the encouragement of the use of the library as a teaching medium. While this applies particularly to school libraries and libraries of colleges and universities, there is plenty of evidence to show the important work in this field which is being carried out by the public libraries.

8 The final objective follows somewhat from the previous one, that is, to encourage among readers a habit of self-instruction; to

do this by giving library users an understanding of search techniques, and by showing them how to gain information on a topic in depth.

In previous chapters we have examined various ways which have been used by working libraries to achieve these objectives. It may be helpful to look at these objectives again and to see what means libraries have used to reach them.

The first aim is to answer the readers' query, what can the library do for me? In general this information is supplied by some form of handout or guide. In some libraries, especially those of teaching institutions, the printed information is reinforced by a library tour, possibly preceded by a film or a tape recorded commentary illustrated by slides. The information for borrowers is of two kinds, the semi-permanent information about the book stock and the services provided by the library, and the less permanent information about the conditions for use and the borrowing arrangements for books and other library materials. This secondary information is often made available by libraries in the form of cards or bookmark slips of paper. When there is a systems approach to exploitation, we have seen how readers can be made aware of what the library has to offer by means of contents panels which can be seen by the reader whenever he or she visits the library. This information may also be seen in several different places in the library, and the broad outlines of information can lead the reader on to more precise items of information. Lastly, information which is temporary involves the idea of change or development, and we have seen how such changes can be announced in broad terms on a notice board. Such brief announcements can then be followed up by means of a printed leaflet to give the required detail.

The second purpose of the exploitation program is to answer the reader's query, where can I find what the library has to offer? Again we have seen that printed guides are much concerned with this problem. Usually, the method used is to show by means of a floor plan the position of all major book collections and the most important library services. Many libraries also have such floor plans displayed at the entrance to the library. Various electronic devices have been used to pin-point desired positions on the plan by means of coloured lights and similar devices. The information on all floor plans depends for its effectiveness on the reader's memory. It is necessary to visualise the information on a complicated drawing and some time later to interpret the information in the form of rooms and book stacks. As an alternative we have seen how a system of colour coded guiding can lead a reader to the desired area by means of overhead signals. No effort of memory is required for this kind of guiding and the route to the desired area may begin from any position in the library.

In the printed library guides which we discussed in the last chapter, the sections of the guide indicated broadly the way in which the library was organised and we have already noted that many of these publications included floor plans. However, there was not generally any discussion of the principles behind the organisation of the library and its contents. In any self-service guiding scheme, an understanding of the thinking behind the organisation of the library is important. It has already been shown how the readers can be made aware of this aspect of the exploitation plan by the layout of the various contents panels and by colour coded guiding. This aspect of guidance can also be emphasised by the layout of the printed guides; and, in one instance by the sequence of the scenes in a film.

Most of the more detailed guides which we have discussed have included instructions for the use of the reference books and bibliographic aids.

Within an exploitation system, we have noted that there are three levels of guidance. First, there is brief visual instruction in the form of wall panels. This method can be used to explain how to use the classification scheme and the catalogue; also, to introduce the use of abstracts and periodicals indexes. Secondly, this outline information is extended and given in greater detail by reader-operated *information stations* where pre-recorded instruction may be received by the reader whenever required. Lastly, there is a series of printed guides which include detailed instructions for using the bibliographic aids in the library.

Another factor is that many people, using bibliographic aids, are aware of the major indexing services, but do not know of the many specialised abstracts and current awareness services which are in the library. In an exploitation system, it is one purpose of the printed guides to give this information. Although the fifth purpose of the program, that of extending the reader's library experience, is likely to be served mostly through his or her personal contact with members of the library staff, the listing of abstracts titles in a library guide is one other way that this may in part be achieved.

There are many examples of how libraries use their readers' special interests to bring about a wider use of books. In the public libraries we are familiar with the various booklists for people with *hobbies*, ' Books for gardeners ', ' Do it yourself books ', etc; also the displays of books to accompany important events in the town, flower shows, civic anniversaries, etc. Other examples include the book and literature displays during scientific conferences at colleges and universities, and also the subject bibliographies prepared by library staff on similar occasions. The purpose of all these booklets and displays is to suggest to the enthusiast and the specialist that he will be able to get more satisfaction from his job or his hobby by using books, whether he is an electronics engineer or a householder wanting to lay a few bricks. As many librarians know, this feeling about books is often equally lacking in both types of enthusiast.

A great deal has been written about the library as a teaching medium. All librarians are familiar with the concept of the ' library college ',[1] and Dr R T Bottle, a chemist, wrote in 1967 : 'As the amount of knowledge increases and one comes to realise just how transient some of the experimental techniques which one uses are, one feels that it might be better to teach students only how to use the literature effectively and to let them educate themselves through using it (under guidance) . . . so that the college is the library and the library is the college, with the lecture room ceasing to be the centre of learning, and permitting each student to study independently at his own pace in the library '.[2]

However, librarians in colleges and universities will know that comparatively few lecturers think of libraries in this way, although in modern education, at all levels, students are encouraged to pursue independent lines of enquiry. Project work in the schools has greatly increased, and in the training of teachers in Britain more emphasis has been placed upon their use of libraries. It will be remembered too, that one public library guide, discussed in the last chapter, was aimed specifically at school teachers.

In encouraging a habit of self-instruction among library users, personal contact between the librarian and the reader is important but, as Professor Knapp[3] and others[4] have found, a much more important factor in academic institutions is the attitude of teachers and the requirements of the teaching program. Within an exploitation system this objective can only be approached through the closest co-operation between the librarian and the teachers.

PHYSICAL ORGANISATION OF DOCUMENTS AND SERVICES

Basic to the design of any program for making the resources of a library accessible to its readers is the policy or thinking behind the physical arrangement of the documents and services in it. For this reason, before discussing the maintenance and up-dating routines which are necessary to keep an exploitation program running smoothly, it may be useful to consider very briefly some of these principles.

In every exploitation program the purpose of this organisation is simply to make the library as easy as possible to use. All the other aims of the program follow from this one.

Perhaps the first principle behind the grouping of books and services is that material to be used by any single group of readers should be kept together; thus, in a public library there is almost always one collection of books for children and another one for adults, while in university libraries there is an increasing tendency to keep the books for undergraduates separate from those for academic staff and people taking postgraduate courses or doing research.

The next concern is to establish a logical pattern. This pattern may be expressed in several ways. The form of the material may be the criterion which decides the organisation method; as an example, in an academic or research library it is often convenient to keep the periodicals together, the assumption being that periodical information is likely to be used mostly by people following up specific references which may range over many titles or many subjects. Some libraries prefer a strict subject arrangement, so that books, periodicals and pamphlets on the same subject are filed together. This arrangement can present some difficulties; for example, periodicals tend to cover a wide range of subjects, which makes them more difficult to classify than books; and the pamphlets need some kind of physical protection before being filed in ordinary book shelves. To overcome these difficulties, some college and university libraries have used a modification of a strict subject approacr to the arrangement of library materials by setting up *subject departments*. Such divisions are broad and usually based upon subject areas corresponding to the divisions of the classification scheme which is used for arranging books in the library. Each such *subject department* then becomes almost a library in miniature, so that within the subject area are kept the books, the pamphlets and the periodicals together with a catalogue and the relevant literature guides, bibliographies, abstracts and periodicals indexes. The arrangement is probably *more* convenient for *most* of the readers.

There are, of course, disadvantages. Courses and disciplines tend to overlap the subjects grouped in the departments. There is some tendency also for students of courses based mainly within one department to ignore information in the other subject departments. A third way of arranging library materials systematically is to base the organisation upon the requirements of search techniques. As an example, the catalogue, all bibliographic aids and general reference books may be kept together in one area, the assumption being that a search will begin with information in general reference sources, and will then move to a search of the catalogue to determine the books and pamphlet material likely to be useful. Lastly, references to information in periodicals and reports will be obtained by using the bibliographic aids.

SPECIAL COLLECTIONS

Finally, there are special collections of books and other materials generally used by a small number of readers, which may deal with many subjects, but which have an added value because the collection is complete and kept together. There are many examples of such collections. The most familiar are possibly the local history and area-interest collections which are found in so many public libraries. Collections of documents of this kind, of particular interest in academic libraries, are the official publications of the central and local government authorities.

In all the larger college and university libraries, the collections of these official publications are an important information source. An awareness of government activity and of how this activity is recorded in official publications is important to students of all kinds, and matters dealing with various aspects of education have a special interest for teachers.

Some librarians argue that Her Majesty's Stationery Office and the publishers of official documents outside Britain are ' just like any other publishers ', and that therefore the official documents should be incorporated into the library stock in the normal way. These publications are, of course, mainly of interest in their countries of origin; but many official reports have an important bearing on a large number of subjects. Relevant information is often to be found most easily by rapid browsing. Very frequently, information in one publication refers back to information in a previous official publication. This information can be followed up most easily when the documents are filed nearby.

A practical consideration is that the completeness of a collection of this kind is an important factor in its usefulness; and, by filing the various command papers etc in sequence, checking of the library's holdings is much simpler. HMSO and other official publishers issue catalogues with various cumulations, which are useful for tracing information in official publications. There is also a number of published guides explaining the use of official publications. Such guides are particularly useful to people consulting these documents, if available in the official publications area. Details of some of these published guides are included in the list of guides at the end of chapter 4.

ROUTINES FOR MAINTAINING AN EXPLOITATION SYSTEM

As always, the simplest routines are the most valuable to the reader. Shelf labels are the visual aids most helpful in saving the reader's time.

SHELVING BOOKS

In order to make the book stock of the library readily accessible to readers, the regular checking of book shelves to keep the books in the correct classified order is probably the most important routine. Coupled with this duty is the need to arrange for returned books to be replaced on the shelves as rapidly as possible. It can be assumed that the most-needed books will be most frequently borrowed. One way of lessening this difficulty is to have a small section of shelving in the main areas of the library where recently returned books can be shelved in roughly classified groups. For example, assuming a classification by Dewey in the social sciences, all books beginning 30 . . . could be on one shelf, those beginning 31 . . . on the next shelf, and so on. Readers can rapidly scan a single shelf for a required book, while little extra time is taken by the assistant in roughly sorting a batch of books before shelving in the *Recently returned* shelves. When eventual filing of the books is made in the main shelves, the process can be considerably speeded up by having the books already partly sorted.

SHELF LABELS

As part of shelving procedures it will be necessary to check the position of shelf labelling. For this reason labels should be easily moveable. It will at the same time be necessary to check that stack end information is relevant.

In maintaining permanent visual information there are two variable factors: the short-term minor changes in contents panels and in the guiding signal arrangements; and the inevitable expansions in book stock, and the consequent major changes in position of books and services. The more specific the contents information, the more likely it is to change. For example, the contents label listing abstracts shelved in a section of the library will need to be changed when new titles are added to the abstract holdings. For this reason, the library needs label holders that allow the simple replacement of an old label by a new one.

For small changes of stock position, dummy books are a useful device. For example, in a *subject department* library, it was decided to remove the German dictionaries for engineers from the department holding German language material to that which held the books and periodicals in engineering. A dummy book with an appropriate label was a simple way of informing readers, in the German language area, of this change. When changes are made in the location of larger groups of books and other material, bold overhead signs are most helpful. For example, in the same library it became necessary to move the position of the book stack housing the *oversize books*. Many readers overlook this material, so that it is helpful to label it plainly. After the change, the original hanging sign was taken to the new position and replaced by one announcing the new arrangement.

INSTRUCTION PANELS AND LABELS

The information on instruction labels and panels may not change, but the position of the relevant catalogues and equipment often does. Routine checking is necessary to see that when equipment is moved or new equipment is installed, appropriate instructions panels are set up.

MAJOR CHANGES IN VISUAL INFORMATION

In the library to which reference has been made above, it was found that after two years, some modification of the hanging signs was necessary. The main contents panels were unaltered, but some of the information on the contents panels for the departments needed to be changed; the positions of several of the hanging signs were altered; and the detailed information was changed. These modifications were made more easily as the lettering on these signs and panels was in *Letraset* (transfer letters) on perspex sheet. It was possible for the signwriter to clean off the detail which had become out-of-date and to add the necessary modifications to the original panel.

Printed guides: Taking as an example those described at the end of the last chapter, the single sheet guide contains brief information about the organisation of the library and the services which it can offer. This type of information requires up-dating at least once a year. The more specific guides contain two kinds of information: *notes* on how readers can find and use various kinds of information; and *contents* information, for example, the periodicals held by the library. This contents information changes and requires up-dating, especially that relating to the holdings of periodicals and bibliographic aids.

Periodicals holdings information can be kept up to date by issuing supplements to the main list. One method of doing this, suitable for small or medium sized libraries, is to record details of new periodical titles on a strip index on which items may be easily kept in an alphabetical sequence. By photocopying the index each month, supplementary lists can be simply produced which can then be inserted into the periodicals guide.

Each month the existing supplement is removed and the new one takes its place. These supplements eventually become unwieldy and it is necessary to bring the complete list up-to-date. For the very many temporary handouts the most important updating routine is to see that obsolete information is removed from circulation. Brief mention has been made of the special collections of official publications. While accessioning procedure is not part of the exploitation program, much of the usefulness of certain collections is reduced if gaps in them develop. For this reason a routine check of the completeness of holdings is part of a program to bring about a wider use of the collection.

Finally, in any self-service system, various mechanical devices need regular servicing. This applies particularly to machines for transmitting pre-recorded instruction which are operated by the reader, and to much-used equipment such as photocopiers. Daily checks are necessary to maintain an efficient service.

PERSONAL CONTACT BETWEEN READERS
AND LIBRARY STAFF

LIBRARY INSTRUCTION: A great deal has been written about the form and content of library instruction in colleges and universities. In 1966, the writer made a survey[4] of the library instruction which was being given in the colleges and universities of Britain, and also in some similar libraries in USA. At that time this instruction was being given at three levels:

1 *Introductory*; the objectives, at this level, were:

(*a*) A tour of the library, leading to an awareness of library facilities, rules and organisation. The average time taken was 30 to 60 minutes.

(*b*) Some instruction in using the catalogue, and possibly general bibliographies and periodicals indexes, which included very little student participation. Sometimes this instruction, which lasted from one to two hours, included a short library assignment; but members of the teaching staff were not usually involved.

2 *A systematic study of information sources*, which occasionally led to an exercise in finding specific information. The time for the course was two to six hours. There was considerable participation by students, and the teaching staff often played some part.

3 *Courses in finding and using information*, which included a literature search, extensive reading, and the selection and evaluation of information for a specific purpose. Results of the search were presented as a written report and an oral paper. An essential ingredient of such courses was a close association between the librarian and the academic staff. These courses varied in length from twelve to thirty hours. Maximum student participation was assumed, and the library course was closely integrated into the general teaching plan. The teaching embodied an element which

115

evaluated the results of the instruction. That is to say, at each stage of the course students completed a library exercise to show that the relevant instruction had been understood and could be applied in a practical way.

As has already been mentioned, this library instruction did not have the hoped-for results. Although it is a simple matter to show students how to use the catalogue and a variety of bibliographic aids, or even to search realistically for information in depth, when the library course ends, a high proportion of students makes little further use of the library.

During the survey, criticism came from students on two counts; first, that library instruction was not necessary to their studies, and secondly that, if it were necessary, it seldom came at the right time. Teachers' comment depended a good deal on the subject taught and upon the teaching methods used by individual teachers; but many considered simply that students should read recommended texts, and that, at least for undergraduates, library instruction was unnecessary. These people also made the point that students needed all their time for the study of examination subjects. The most comprehensive assessment of the effect of library instruction upon the way students use the library was carried out by the late Prof Knapp at Monteith College of Wayne State University.[3] The Monteith experiments showed, first, that the students' attitude toward library instruction reflected the attitudes of their teachers; and secondly, that if the teaching program required the use of the library, the library was used; but, when this motivation was not present, most students made little use of books apart from standard texts.

In a comprehensive exploitation program, library instruction is one other way of training a reader to use information in the library. The purpose is more to involve the reader in the library organisation and to show how the machinery works, than to transmit to him details of library techniques. In this way, the reader can, at any time, operate that part of the machinery which fulfils his or her immediate library requirement. While the pattern of instruction is not greatly altered, the supporting elements are more permanent, and continue to be used during the subsequent personal contact between members of the library staff and the individual readers.

At this point it may be helpful to look at the program followed at the library with which the writer is most familiar. Class instruction is still being given at the three levels mentioned above, although the time occupied by the most comprehensive courses is now much shorter, and courses, even at the second level, are only offered when library instruction is an integral part of the teaching program. A large proportion of the students at the beginning of the year receive an introductory library talk, see the library film and make a brief tour of the library.

In general the talk is based upon the information in the single sheet guide. The principles behind the organisation of the library are given some emphasis, and the self-help aspects of the library service are explained. The film, the script for which is included in chapter 3, is designed to show how the library user, by reading coloured signals, is able to find the book or the information he needs.

During the tour, the emphasis is placed rather upon *where to find out* than *how to use* information. For example, the main contents panels on the stair landings are pointed out as a first source of information to show how the library is organised and the facilities it has to offer. Also, as the students at this polytechnic are familiar with the colour coded lights in the London underground railway stations, which are used to direct travellers to the different platforms, colour as a guiding device is not a new idea.

All librarians who have attempted to show a touring group how to use the catalogue will know the problems involved, and how few of the group remember any of the instruction which has been given. There is no difficulty, however, in pointing out, even to the largest group, that there are four aids to help readers wishing to use the catalogue: the main instruction panel on the wall above the catalogue; on each cabinet, a standing label which describes the purpose of that part of the catalogue and the entries contained in it; *the catalogue information station,* where, at the flick of a switch, a reader may receive detailed instruction whenever it is needed; and lastly, the printed information in the guide, *How to find out.*

At the entrance to each department is a rack of *Aids to finding information in the library* containing guides and leaflets. This information is pointed out as another way of finding out about the library when the need arises. The general principle behind this introductory session of a little over half an hour is to leave students with a feeling of an understanding of the library machine without the need to remember detailed information for which they have no immediate use. As a reminder of the library tour, each student has a single-sheet guide which can be read in two minutes or less.

In the more comprehensive courses, detailed instruction is based upon the notes in the printed guides discussed in chapter 4. The topics covered in the course fall into six groups:

1 *The organisation of information in libraries*: library co-operation and interloan; library classification and the catalogue.

2 *The organisation of information in books and periodicals* : evaluating a book for a given purpose; quick reference books; information in various types of periodical.

3 *Bibliographic aids*: bibliographies, periodicals indexes, abstracts, review series, subject guides.

4 *Special areas of information*: British government publications, research organisations, patent specifications and British Standard specifications.

5 *Literature searching techniques*: gathering information, recording references.

6 *Presenting the results of the search*: writing a report; giving an oral paper.

Details for individual courses depend upon the needs of the students involved and the time available for instruction. All students have a copy of each guide for use in the class, but these guides are not distributed free. The guides may be purchased for a nominal price of five pence, but reference copies are to be found in several places in each department of the library.

In shorter courses, particular emphasis is placed upon the use of the catalogue, especially as a means of finding information on a specific subject. At this time, the pre-recorded instruction at the *information stations* is a useful teaching aid for a member of a class who has for some reason missed a time-tabled session when the use of the catalogue is discussed and when each student had an opportunity to make practical use of the catalogue.

The second most important part of the course is concerned with teaching the use of abstracts and periodicals indexes as a means of gathering references in a literature search; and, once again, the relevant information station may be used for individual students as a substitute for instruction in a live class. During a literature search students come upon a number of common problems in understanding the information given in abstracts and periodicals indexes. In class discussion, hypothetical examples of these difficulties have little significance, but it is hoped that by supporting such discussion with reference back to sections of a printed guide, the student will be aware, when a practical difficulty arises, of a ready source of information which may help to solve the problem.

LIBRARY STAFF ADVICE TO READERS

As part of the exploitation program, it is intended that the instruction given in library classes will be extended by individual contacts; the details will be decided by the circumstances of the meeting.

All readers' advisers know that the first difficulty in helping readers is to find out what the enquirer really wants to know, and then, at what level the information will be useful. Very often the clue to the reader's real need comes from discovering what purpose the requested information will serve when found. All college librarians have experienced these difficulties: the student who is seeking articles on the ' psychology of dyslexia ', who asks whether the library has any books ' on reading '; and the reader who asks for *The marine engineers handbook* when information is needed on diesel engines.

This aspect of the readers advisory work is not altered, but the general pattern of help will be to support the advice given to a reader by directing him back to the elements in the system which are likely to be helpful. The student needing information on dyslexia can be directed to the information about abstracts in the printed guide. The abstract titles likely to aid in the search can be pointed out and the suggestion made that the *information station* may be helpful if the reader is unfamiliar with the use of abstracts. In practice, the response to such an enquiry would probably include some practical demonstration of the use of abstract information, as well as a reference of the reader back to the elements of the self-service system.

Similarly, in giving help to someone wishing to use the catalogue, attention can be directed to the wall panel instructions, to the section of the guide dealing with the catalogue, and to the pre-recorded instruction available at the turn of a switch. The commonest use of the catalogue is to find books by a known author, frequently from *required reading* lists. When advice is sought on these occasions, there is an opportunity to point out the other ways of using the catalogue. This approach to reader advice has two advantages. The reader receives help in a form which does not require any effort of memory, and the library staff have a set of aids which will save time and will simplify the process of communication with the reader. The printed guides also serve to remind the library adviser of sources of information which can be used in solving enquiries of various kinds. For example, it is often helpful to know which abstracts are received by the library or which review series are in the shelves. This type of gathered information is not readily available from the catalogue or other library records.

LIBRARY LIAISON WITH ACADEMIC STAFF

In a teaching institution, the chief purpose of the library is to aid the teaching and learning program. The more closely the library is integrated into the teaching arrangements, the more effective is the role of the library. Several experiments, especially those of Professor Knapp, have shown that a wider use of libraries by students in their learning program depends upon the teaching needs. Therefore, if the library in a college or a university is to play its full part in the teaching program, liaison between the library and the academic staff is a particularly important activity. Academic staff are first of all individual readers who use the library in various ways. Some come to the library to gather information in pursuit of their special interests; others are also doing research and preparing articles and books for publication. Almost all lecturers use the library in preparing their course lectures. The teaching staff also plan library activity into the program for the students.

This activity is of three kinds:

Reading lists: Almost all courses require students to read certain books. These reading lists are usually handed to the students at the beginning of the academic year. The bibliographic detail on these lists is often scanty. Generally such lists are handed to students without consultation with the library. At the beginning of each year, it is a common sight to see in the library students following up information in reading lists, trying to trace the information in the catalogue.

As part of the liaison program, these lists prepared by academic staff can be checked by library staff for bibliographic detail, and entries can then be set down in some recognised library form, including the classmark and other location symbols. When the information is correct, the lists may be returned to the lecturer to arrange for the necessary duplication; or the library can arrange for the printing to be done.

This co-operation between the library and the teaching staff has a number of advantages. The library is made aware in good time of the books which will be needed; and, as the bibliographic detail is correct, the library staff will be saved the time taken in tracing for students books with incomplete detail. The lecturer will know that the necessary books are in the library in sufficient numbers, and that students will be able to find the books on the shelves with the least waste of time.

Reserved book collection: Reserved book collections are a well known feature in very many university libraries and in a growing number of college libraries. They are an important factor in exploiting the resources in a library. The items included in a reserved book collection are the books, reports and articles selected as *recommended* or *required* reading for students in various courses. Some of the texts are more or less permanently reserved in this way, other items may be reserved for a few weeks or months. The arrangements for readers to borrow from the collection vary with the needs of different libraries. In general, the books may be used only in the library or borrowed overnight. Some libraries restrict the period of loan to two hours even for use within the library, and impose a heavy fine for keeping the book longer than the permitted period. In one university in USA the fine for an overdue book begins at one dollar for the first hour overdue.

In every academic library the main complaint from readers is that the book needed is ' out '. This difficulty is greatly reduced if at least one copy of the required reading texts is to be found in the reserved book collection. The reserved texts can be marked in the catalogue, but it is extremely helpful to readers if, in addition, lists of reserved texts can be available in several places in the library. In a small or medium sized library these lists can be kept on a strip index. The entries on the index can then be arranged in the required order and photocopied at regular intervals to obtain sufficient copies to inform readers in various parts of the library. Since these books are usually identified by their authors, a list arranged in order of authors provides the most useful information for readers.

There are many advantages in having a reserved book collection. The lecturer can be sure that at least one copy of a recommended text will be ' in the library '. The students can have similar confidence. The work of library staff will be reduced, since there will be fewer frustrated readers and fewer requests for books which are ' out '.

Of course, the reserved book collection has to be controlled, and space must be allocated for it. In small and medium sized libraries reserved books are usually shelved behind the library counter. Some of the larger university libraries have a special reserved book room with a study area attached to it. A simple system for borrowing includes a book card inserted in a long clear plastic envelope which is filed with each book. When a loan is arranged, the borrower enters on the book card his name, date, and other details. The book card is then placed in the envelope which is put on the shelf in place of the book. In this way, the books which have been borrowed can be identified at a glance.

Projects: As part of the library liaison program, it is important to know in advance of any proposed special studies or projects which are to be carried out by students, and which will include the use of the library. There are two ways that library aid may be sought. It may be necessary to arrange courses in library instruction for a group of students; and, there may be gaps to be filled in the library holdings of required literature; or, some duplication of the items already held by the library may be desirable.

SOME PROBLEMS IN ARRANGING LIBRARY LIAISON WITH ACADEMIC STAFF

Arrangements for liaison can never be very clear cut. The individual attitudes of members of the academic staff towards the library is always a governing factor. Some people will be much more willing to co-operate in the ways suggested than others. With all teaching staff it may be difficult to arrange times to meet for the purpose of discussing the several aspects of the liaison program. The problems are different in different institutions, but a systematic approach to library liaison can help to reduce some of these difficulties.

The first need is for the library staff involved to realise what liaison with the teaching staff is setting out to achieve. Broadly, there are three objectives: first, to establish the confidence of the academic staff in the service of the library; secondly, to make simpler the closer integration of library use into the teaching program; and lastly, to save time for the people involved, the teachers and the students who wish to use the library, and the library staff who are providing the necessary services to them.

Gaining the confidence and goodwill of the teaching staff is an essential starting point for any liaison program. It depends mostly upon the service which individual lecturers have received from the library. Perhaps the most important purpose that liaison can serve in this respect is to follow up complaints which arise and without unnecessary delay. On occasion very small changes in library routine can make a great deal of difference to attitudes. The writer recalls an experience in a college library some years ago. It was the practice of this library to lend periodicals to teaching staff as required. The complaint from the academic staff in one department was that the required periodicals were always on loan. This particular problem was solved when about twenty periodical titles, those most in demand, were reserved for use only in the library. Articles in these periodicals, which the lecturers wished to retain, were photocopied at the expense of the department.

To make integration simpler for the people who teach, it is necessary for them to know how the library can help the teaching program; by providing the necessary books, by establishing restricted borrowing arrangements for heavily used texts; and by arranging courses of instruction for students.

As a means of saving time for library staff and for teachers it will be helpful if the library services required for teaching purposes can be recorded on a standard form which is processed through a central point in the library. An example of such a form is given on page 125. Although there is always some reluctance to fill in forms, there are several advantages in using a record of this nature. Much of the cause of poor library service comes from bad communication between the reader and the library staff— the failure of the library to find out what the reader needs, and of the reader to supply sufficient information to enable the library to obtain what is wanted. In this situation the library wishes to give a good service and the reader is very willing to give the necessary information. One way of meeting these problems is to use carefully designed forms or stationery where there is a space allotted for the various items of required information. The *Library liaison record* reminds the lecturer of the details which are needed by the library to give him what he wants. It is also a good deal quicker to use a standard form, rather than to send requests for library service on odd scraps of paper or by telephone messages.

Finally, when discussion between lecturers and library liaison

LIBRARY LIAISON RECORD

The PURPOSE of this record is to integrate the library staff more closely into the TEACHING PROGRAMME by giving EARLY WARNING of student needs:-

(1) By listing BASIC TEXTS needed for courses. (These texts are those which ALL students will require to use, and to which reference is made in lectures).

(2) By giving notice of INDIVIDUAL PROJECTS to be set for students.

(3) By giving notice of any other matters calling for LIBRARY CO-OPERATION.

I.   COLLEGE COURSES - BASIC TEXTS

COURSE NUMBER.............................

LECTURER'S SUBJECT ....

NUMBER OF STUDENTS ....

PERIOD for which texts will be required : From .... To ....

(Are these texts required throughout the whole period of the course or for a limited period?)

SHORT TERM LOAN etc	AUTHOR (Please PRINT the names)	Short Title	Date	Publisher	Price

II. INDIVIDUAL PROJECTS·

COURSE NUMBER.............................

SUBJECT(S) of project ....

NUMBER of STUDENTS ....

PERIOD the project will cover : From .... To ....

TEXTS to be placed on SHORT TERM LOAN:-

AUTHOR (Please PRINT Names)	Title	Date

III.   OTHER MATTERS for attention:-

staff takes place, if it is based upon the information in a standard 'record', the detailed requirements for a particular course or a particular book or publication are less likely to be overlooked. For the library, it is always easier to transfer information to the various records of the library if it is supplied in a standard form. When, for instance, bibliographic detail is incomplete it is immediately obvious and can be simply added to the entry on the *record* after consultation with a standard bibliography.

The advantages of passing the library liaison information through a central point in the library are, first, that a general picture of liaison activity is presented, so that a better coverage can be made of the academic staff, who may not be making the expected use of the library; secondly, the necessary control of books, etc is simpler. Very frequently the same text-book is reserved for use with several courses. Such information could indicate a need to order extra copies of the book.

As with other aspects of the exploitation scheme, perhaps the most important function of the library liaison staff is to inform academic staff of the services available to them, and to explain how the exploitation system works.

REFERENCES

1 L Shores and others: *The library college* ... Drexel Institute, 1966.

2 R T Bottle: 'Training students to use scientific and technical information', in R E Collison: *Progress in library science.* Butterworth, 1967.

3 P B Knapp: *Experiment in co-ordination between teaching and library staff for changing student use of library resources.* Detroit, Wayne State University, 1964.

4 R J P Carey: *Teaching and tutorial activities of librarians with students not training for the library profession.* FLA thesis, Library Assn, 1966.

6

Materials and equipment

PRACTICAL CONSIDERATIONS: When carrying out a guiding program there is a number of practical matters to be considered with respect to the materials, the techniques and the fittings which will be used to produce the hardware for the system. Final selection of hardware will depend upon the type of library, its size and the premises which it occupies, but the majority of librarians are short of funds, have less staff than they need to do the things they would like to do, and they are always pressed for time. Although a great deal of money may be spent on a guiding system, these notes have been included to show that effective guiding can be put into a library in a short time and with inexpensive materials. Also, since libraries are not static organisations, great durability for guiding information and materials is not the most important consideration; and, even in a large library with ample funds, it is advisable to begin by installing a temporary scheme using cheap materials and rapid methods of production.

PERMANENT VISUAL INFORMATION
The basic requirements for designing the various wall panels, signs, and labels which carry the permanent visual information are:

1 A sheet material with a suitable printing surface.

2 Printing materials and techniques.

3 Coloured signal materials.

4 Protection for the printing surface when the visual information has been applied to it.

5 Physical support and display fittings.

There are five types of guiding unit:

1 *Wall panels* for supplying contents information at various levels of detail, and instructions for using the catalogue and

other library equipment (microfilm readers, photocopiers, etc). Examples are illustrated in plate 5, nos 3, 12.

2 *Standing panels.* These supply similar information to that on the wall panels. They are usually smaller in area than wall panels and are self supporting. They may be placed on any horizontal surface. Examples are shown in plate 5, no 6.

3 *Overhead direction signs.* These signs carry large coloured signals, about six inches in diameter, with brief information about each signal area. They are possibly most effective when suspended from the ceiling at about eight feet from floor level. Alternatively these signs may be in the form of a standing panel, or may jut out from the top of a high book stack using a cantilever support. Some examples are illustrated in plate 5, nos 1, 7, 9, 11.

4 *Label holders.* Certain guiding information in a developing library may change frequently. One simple way of keeping this information up to date is to use a label holder with a removable label which can easily be replaced. As information becomes outdated, the old label is removed and a new label is inserted in its place. In practice two standard holders have proved useful; one is ten inches square, the other is rectangular, ten inches deep and eighteen inches long. This type of holder can be screwed to a wall, a book stack end or any other vertical surface; or, the fitting may be constructed as a free standing unit. See plate 5, nos 10, 13.

5 *Shelf label fittings.* There is a number of types of shelf label holders available from library suppliers. In general, the unit comprises a tongue, which lies horizontally on the shelves under the books, with a vertical lip which lies against the edge of the shelf and has a slot for the label. These units are made in both metal and plastic. Label holders may be moved from shelf to shelf as required. Perhaps the most satisfactory shelf label holding facility is a running slot along the full length of the shelf which is incorporated into the shelf structure. With this type of shelving the moving of a label from one shelf to another may be a little more difficult, but using the tool described below it is possible to move and replace the same label many times. The completely mobile tongued label holder tends to come loose from the shelves and to fall out of place.

Tool for removing shelf labels. On the shelves described above, the label holder comprises a hollow slot with turned in edges. In the slot is a thin metal strip approximately $\frac{3}{4}$ inch wide and resting on a backing of foamed plastic about $\frac{3}{8}$ inch thick. This compressible strip holds the shelf label firmly in place against the turned in edges of the slot, so that it is difficult to remove a label without tearing it. However, this can be done quite easily with a tool made from a piece of flat steel which is approximately $\frac{1}{8}$ inch thick and $\frac{1}{2}$ inch wide and bent at right angles at one end to form an ' L ' shape. The flat tongue of the tool, which should be rather longer than the label, can be slid behind it by compressing the backing strip and then by turning the tool through a quarter circle the loosened label can be flicked out of the slot without damage.

Dummy books. Most librarians are familiar with these guiding aids, which, as the name suggests, are simply boxes made of card, wood or plastic in the shape of a book. Library suppliers offer various types, some of which have a slot on the spine to hold a replaceable label.

PRODUCING THE HARDWARE

At the present time any librarian proposing to put a guiding system into a library will have to design much of his own necessary hardware. As yet library suppliers have not produced all the fittings which are needed.

PRINTING SURFACE MATERIALS

(*a*) Paper or thin card is the cheapest medium and the most flexible in application. Information on it may be printed, typed, hand-lettered or hand-drawn in any colour. Transfer and adhesive letters may also be used, and the paper may be attached to card or board for physical support. Paper is particularly useful for displaying temporary or short-term information. It can be protected by a transparent film, for example by *transpaseal,* when necessary, and multiple copies in black and white may be readily produced by photocopying. Although paper in very large sizes may be obtained, for practical purposes paper signs and labels will be most suitable on sheets not larger than A4 or foolscap.

(b) *Card*: Stiff card or strawboard covered on one or both sides with white paper can be obtained in large sheets, and is probably the most useful material for temporary and semi-permanent signs. Information may be put upon it in all the ways used for paper except by direct typing and printing. In the preparation of contents panels and direction signs, paper signals may be gummed to the surface of the card. A completed panel can then be protected by an adhesive film. Although a skilled sign-writer may be required to produce a professionally finished sign by hand lettering, any library technician can make an attractively finished sign or panel by using transfer lettering. *Letraset* and other brands of transfer lettering can be purchased in a large number of different sizes. For smaller labels and panels, which are required in quantity, a great deal of time can be saved if the card is cut to the required sizes by the supplier. This is particularly so when preparing card for the two large label holders described above. The chief disadvantage of using card for producing guiding units is its tendency to warp with changes of atmospheric conditions.

(c) *Perspex* can be supplied in various colours and degrees of translucency. *Dense white* perspex sheet is perhaps the most suitable material for large panels and hanging signs in a library. Perspex does not warp, even in large thin sheets, but the densest white sheet is still somewhat translucent. When hung in strong light this causes shadows to show through the double sided signs. Also the surface carries a high polish which reflects the light, so that care is required in placing signs with respect to the lighting in the library. After the lettering on the panel is complete, a permanent unit can be made by fastening a thin sheet of clear perspex over the finished surface. If the edges of the two sheets are then sealed with cement, the unit is completely dust-proof and is protected against surface damage. One cement suitable for this purpose is 'Tensol cement no 6'. Perspex is a strong stiff material, so that a sheet of about $\frac{1}{8}$ inch thickness is suitable even for fairly large signs. For hand-printing coloured signals or for hand-lettering it is necessary to use a specially prepared acrylic paint (*Cerric acrylic paint* is a suitable material). However, transfer lettering such as *Letraset* adheres satisfactorily to the surface of perspex. In common with other plastic materials, perspex attracts dust particles, but this tendency can be considerably reduced by treating the completed sign with an anti-static solution.

(*d*) *Hardboard,* which is made from compressed wood fibres, can be obtained sealed on either side with a white plastic sheet. In this form it is marketed under various trade names. For painting coloured signals or hand-lettering it is necessary to use a signwriters enamel, but transfer lettering adheres well to the plastic surface. It is somewhat less expensive than perspex sheet. The surface has a matt finish, so that there is no problem with reflection. This composite material is completely opaque but it has a tendency to warp slightly.

(*e*) *Painted wood.* One large public library group in London has made a series of moveable signs to fasten above the non-fiction book stacks. These signs, which bear the main Dewey class numbers and the relevant subjects, are on lengths of wooden board about 4 feet long by 6 inches in width. These boards are painted white in a matt finished enamel, with *Letraset* characters in black for the numers and letters. (See plate 4A.)

COLOURED SIGNALS

In a system of guiding, coloured signals are used to indicate specific areas in the library. These signals are arranged so that they may be recognised from a distance, and so that an array of signals can be seen at a glance. For example, a reader who has found out from a contents panel or hanging sign the colour coding for the area he needs, should be able to see at a glance where the required area is located. For this reason, overhead signals need to be large enough to be recognised from anywhere in a library area, and there must be as great a contrast as possible between the colours used. The requirements for coloured signals have already been briefly discussed in chapter 2.

There are two ways that signalled information may be coded,

by the colour of the signal and by its shape. In the writer's experience, five colours, blue, yellow, green, red and dark brown or black, have proved most useful. The contrast is good and five colours can be remembered without effort. Two shapes, squares and circles, have so far supplied sufficient variation in working schemes; but it is suggested that, for a system in a very large library, triangular signals might be included. The general thinking behind the use of shape is that each shape indicates a division of progressively greater detail. For example, five colour coded square signals indicate five different major library areas; five colour coded circular signals indicate five minor areas in each major area; so that five colour coded square signals coupled with five colour coded circular signals may identify twenty five areas in the library. By adding a third shape of signal, one hundred and twenty five areas could be identified.

For permanent signs on perspex or plastic-sealed hardboard, coloured signals need to be painted on to the surface of the panel, but for more temporary signs, signals cut from coloured paper can be attached to a card or paper surface. In Britain, coloured paper cut into squares and circles of various sizes and with an adhesive on one side of the paper is used widely in schools. This precut sticky paper saves a great deal of time in preparing the panels and signs for a temporary scheme of guiding.

PRINTING TECHNIQUES

The technique chosen to put information on to panels and signs will depend upon the purpose of the sign, and whether the sign is to remain as a permanent guiding element.

Felt pens: The quickest way of lettering a sign for an amateur is to use a felt or fibre tipped pen. Pens with tips of various widths are available in several colours. Felt pen lettering of this kind is particularly suitable for roughing out the signs and panels for a temporary guiding scheme. If a felt pen is used with a stencil, a little more time will be needed, but the quality of the printing will be improved.

Transfer lettering is a process in which the printed characters (letters, numbers and symbols) are transferred from a transparent backing on to the required printing surface, which may be paper, card, perspex, plastic sheet or painted wood, etc. There is an adhesive on the back of the letter which when placed in position is transferred by rubbing the transparent backing with some smooth rounded point such as a soft lead pencil. When the transfer lettering is complete, it is necessary to fix the characters in place by spraying them with a sealing compound. By using this process, panels and signs may be produced with a professional finish by people unskilled in hand-lettering. If changes in guiding information are made, transfer letters may be removed from a hard surface such as perspex or plastic sheet and the required modification can be made comparatively easily and quickly.

Adhesive letters of various kinds are available. They are of different colours, thicknesses and materials. In general, these letters are coated on the under surface with an adhesive which is covered by a backing material. To use the letters, the backing is stripped off and the letter is placed on the printing surface and pressed into position. Such letters are useful when bold headings are required on a sign or panel. One series of such letters on thin polyvinyl sheet gives an effect similar to printing.

Typewritten script: This is the commonest way of producing information for library readers. All librarians are familiar with the standard machines, but some may not know of a very simple modification, namely the *bulletin typewriter*. This machine types only upper case letters and numbers. The characters, which are larger than upper case letters on a standard machine and in heavier type, make much more effective labels and other guiding information than is possible with a standard typewriter.

Photographic copying: It is a characteristic of a systems guiding scheme that the same information may be displayed in several places in the library. Photographic techniques are particularly suitable for producing multiple copies of a guiding element, for example, of a contents panel; also for producing copies for different positions in the library.

In the context of this chapter, photographic copying refers to ordinary black and white photography in which the camera is used to make a negative, from which one or more prints are made using an enlarger. The prints so made may be larger or smaller than the original object photographed, and one photographic negative may be used to print copies of various sizes.

With specialised equipment and materials, very large prints may be made. With the photographic facilities which are likely to be available in a college, prints of about 20 × 16 inches are the largest practicable. However, a single panel may be made from two or more single prints. Very effective signs and panels may also be prepared by photographing a small *master* and enlarging the print to the required size. The master may be prepared on a typewriter, or by using transfer letters, or with any other black and white materials. Such masters can be made very much more quickly than a full size panel.

There are several advantages in using photographic copies of this kind. The contrast between the black of the lettering and the white of the background is very strong; prints of various sizes can be made very rapidly, and the process is a cheap one when compared with the cost of making individual copies of a panel by hand. The most satisfactory way of attaching the print to a card support is by *dry mounting* on a photographic press, and when this is done the print becomes a very sturdy unit. Coloured signals cannot, of course, be simply copied; but signals made of coloured paper may be stuck to the photographic print as described earlier, for the preparation of temporary signs on card. Printing paper with a matt surface is most suitable for guiding units, and, in order to protect the surface of such signs, they may be sealed with a transparent film such as *Transpaseal*.

Shelf labelling: A particular application of photographic copying may be worth mentioning. College and university libraries include in their stock large numbers of periodicals. The preparation of shelf labels for these holdings can be a time consuming operation. Such labels may be very rapidly made photographically using a typewritten master. If the titles are typed in columns on ordinary typing paper, the lettering can be enlarged photographically to the required size to fill a label holder.

In one college library, where the shelves have a built-in continuous label slot, the visible portion of the label is roughly half an inch wide so that the width of the complete label needs to be about $^3/_5$ inch. It was found that by typing titles with one and a half spaces between each, the typescript enlarged to give printed labels of the correct size. When the necessary enlargements had been made, the photographic print was cut into strips to make the labels. Such labels have a very good contrast between the lettering and the background paper; and, titles can be comfortably read by people with normal eyesight, at a distance of twelve feet.

On the shelves with running slots the labels can be inserted very quickly, and using the tool described above the label may be simply removed for use in another position, when, for any reason, a file of periodicals must be moved. Photographic prints have a very durable surface, but if desired, the shelf label prints may be protected by a transparent film before being cut into individual labels.

PROTECTION OF THE PRINTING SURFACE

The purpose of protection is to provide a surface which may be washed or dusted, and which is proof against light knocks or abrasions. Some mention has already been made of methods of protection, but it may be helpful to summarise the various materials which may be used.

Glass is possibly the oldest form of protection for printed information in libraries. All librarians are familiar with its use for this purpose.

Clear perspex sheet is rather more expensive than glass. It is just as transparent, but is easier to use and does not crack easily. No frame is required to support it and perspex sheet can be cut and drilled without difficulty. It can also be cemented to other plastic surfaces to form a dust free unit, as described earlier.

Plastic thin sheet or film: Clear plastic film is available in several thicknesses. Melinex and acetate sheets cut into squares to make slides for an overhead projector are useful for protecting small labels, for example, the labels on a dummy book. This plastic sheeting may also be supplied on rolls in various widths.

Adhesive film: Brief mention of the use of this material has already been made. This film has on one surface an adhesive which is protected by a backing sheet of paper, and is supplied on rolls generally about twenty inches in width. To use the film, the backing sheet is stripped back and the film is smoothed on to the surface to be protected. The film may be applied to almost any printed surface. The physical protection is good for minor knocks and abrasions, and the surface may be dusted or washed if necessary.

Heat sealed plastic film: For this process a sealing machine is required. One such machine is the Plasticmaster Roll Laminator supplied by Photo-me International, Walton-on-Thames. This machine uses two rolls of plastic film with two heated rollers, and operates on single-sheet material only. The sheet for sealing is fed into the machine so that the film from one roll passes under the material for sealing, and the film from the other roll passes over it. The sandwich then passes between the pair of heated rollers under pressure. The plastic is sealed to the surfaces to be protected and the edges of the plastic are also sealed. This process is rather expensive. The protection is physically stronger than with adhesive film. The machine is costly, but some commercial firms will carry out this work at reasonable rates. This process is useful for protecting single-sheet documents and charts on thin card.

Liquid film: Aerosol sprays of clear varnish give some protection and produce surfaces which can be dusted and washed for a limited period.

PHYSICAL SUPPORT FOR PANELS AND SIGNS

The purpose of this support is to provide a method of displaying visual information; to strengthen and stiffen the printing surface; to protect the edges of card, board, etc; and to give the guiding elements a pleasing appearance.

It has already been pointed out that library guiding fittings are not at present available from library suppliers. The support methods and materials discussed in the next few paragraphs have all been tested by the author. The materials are cheap and readily available, and the construction methods are simple. No particular skills are necessary and the work can be carried out on an ordinary table.

Method of support: Guiding signs and panels are supported in three ways. They are suspended from above on chains or cord, they are mounted on a wall, a book stack end or some similar vertical surface, or they form a self-supporting unit to stand on the floor, on a table or on some other horizontal surface. For these purposes four types of fitting are required: a suspension batten, suitable for holding a card sign from the top, framing to stiffen wall signs; an easel type of support for standing signs; and, lastly, label holders which can hold replaceable cards.

Support materials: To construct these fittings three types of material will be found useful.

(*a*) Plywood sheet: (i) $\frac{1}{8}$ inch thick; (ii) $^3/_{16}$ inch thick.

(*b*) Square timber battens, the end section of which is $\frac{1}{2}$ inch square, with a saw cut $\frac{1}{4}$ inch deep and $\frac{1}{8}$ inch wide along the middle of one side of the batten. The appearance of the various fittings will be improved if, before being cut up, the battens are painted or sealed with a clear varnish. See plate 5, no 18.

(*c*) U shaped plastic extrusion moulding. This material is sold by 'do-it-yourself' shops to be used as guides for sliding doors. The gap between the shoulders of the 'U' is $^3/_{16}$ inch. See plate 5, no 17.

Edge support: This type of support is used with stiff card. To prepare the card for suspending from above, a piece of wooden batten the length of the card is cut and the groove in the batten is partly filled with adhesive (ici *Dufix* is suitable and is colourless when dry). When the adhesive has been run into the groove, the card is pressed into it. As soon as the adhesive is dry, a screw eye can be screwed into the batten near either end. The unit may then be suspended by light chain or nylon line. See plate 5, nos 9, 11.

As an alternative to suspension, a similar kind of support can be made for small free standing signs, by attaching a piece of batten of the required length to a square of plywood. A simple method of attaching the batten to the ply is to use a stapling machine. The wire of the staple is finer than that in ordinary tacks or nails, so that there is less chance of splitting the batten; also the stapler is easier to use. The adhesive is applied to the groove in the batten in the way described; but when the card is pressed into the groove, it must be supported in an upright position until the adhesive is set. See plate 5, nos 2, 4, 14, 15, 16. In a variation of this type of support, the batten is fastened to the edge of a piece of timber about 6 inches square and one inch thick. The card is then mounted in the groove of the batten vertically, so that it juts out from the top of a book stack, being supported on a cantilever principle by the weight of the timber. See plate 5, nos 1, 8, 5, 7.

Frames: Frames for card signs may be very simply constructed from the same battens. These are fitted around the sign so that the card enters the groove on all four sides. After the battens have been cut to size the groove is partly filled with adhesive and the battens are pressed back on to the sides of the card. As a temporary holding arrangement during construction, each corner may be secured with six or eight inches of *sellotape*. When the adhesive is dry the unit remains rigid and the sellotape can be removed. Since the edge of the card is secured around its whole perimeter there is little tendency to bend or warp. See plate 5, nos 3, 12.

'*Easel*' *supports*: This very simple type of free-standing support is suitable for most sizes of sign and label. It can be constructed from any stiff sheet material. The most suitable for library purposes are cardboard, hardboard or plywood. In principle the support is tent-shaped and may carry a sign on one side or on both. The width of the support should be slightly less than that of the sign or panel. Small supports, four to six inches in height, may be folded from a single sheet of stiff card. For larger supports, it will be simpler to make the 'tent' from three separate sheets of plywood or cardboard. The support can be constructed quite satisfactorily by joining the edges with adhesive tape. *Sellotape* can be used but a stronger unit results from using an adhesive tape with a thick paper or a cloth backing. If the edges of the plywood or the hardboard are rough, they can be smoothed by rubbing with a piece of coarse sandpaper. For a double sided sign the angles at the base of the stand should be about 70 degrees. When fastening a card sign to this kind of support, a rubber-based adhesive, such as *Copydex*, is suitable. It is comparatively easy to remove the sign if the support is needed for another purpose, and it is simple to rub off any surplus adhesive if it should run over on to the sign during construction. See plate 5, no 6.

Label holders: The use of these fittings has already been discussed at some length. They may be very simply constructed from $^3/_{16}$ inch plywood and ' U ' shaped plastic extrusion moulding. Two sizes will be sufficient for most library purposes: one, 10 inches square and the other 18 inches long by 10 inches deep. If a number of holders are to be made, it will be helpful to have the plywood cut to size by the supplier. The plastic moulding is available in white or black, and the edges of the plywood should be painted to match the plastic before the units are assembled. The moulding can be simply cut with a hack saw, and, since each unit is the same size, time will be saved if the required number of pieces of moulding are cut before assembly begins.

An *impact adhesive* is applied to the surface of one flat side of the ' U ' moulding and around three sides of the plywood base. When partially dry, the moulding is pressed into position on the plywood. See plate 5, nos 10, 13.

AUDIO VISUAL AIDS HARDWARE

In chapter 3 we considered some of the types of audio and visual aids which could be used in exploiting library resources. These included films, film strips, television and various combinations based upon tape recorded instruction illustrated by slides or charts.

The production of film and television aids requires specialised equipment and trained technical assistance, so that information on these techniques is beyond the scope of this manual. However, a large number of librarians are experimenting with tape recordings and charts or slides as a means of making information in their libraries more accessible to the readers, so that it may be helpful to discuss some of the equipment which is being used for this purpose in working libraries.

There are two kinds of program. In one, instruction is recorded on tape, and at appropriate times during that instruction the listener is directed to visual information of some kind. This information may be in the form of a slide, a printed chart, or some document or library aid (for example, the catalogue). The charts or slides are added so that the oral instruction may be reinforced by a visual or practical experience.

In the other type of program, the audio instruction controls automatically the visual information in the form of a slide. At the appropriate point in the audio instruction the visual information appears automatically on a screen. There are several variations of both programs and examples have already been discussed in chapter 3.

Reader-operated tape recordings: In a simple application of this technique, the ' walkabout tape ' used by a university in the north of England, the listener, wearing headphones, carried a battery-operated cassette tape recorder on a shoulder strap. The recorded instruction guided the listener from point to point in the library. As the commentary relative to one part of the library came to an end, the listener was instructed to switch off and to proceed to the next area, when the recording was switched on again. This program served as an alternative to a tour of the library attended by a member of the library staff.

Tape recordings and charts: In a slight variation of this program, Hatfield Polytechnic library uses the following equipment (see plate 3A):

1 *Battery-operated cassette tape-recorder* (machines made by three different manufacturers are used). The recorder is housed in a protective box which is 12 inches long, 8 inches wide and 3 inches deep, and which is screwed to a table top. The recorders

have ' piano key ' switches, three of which can be operated by a reader, viz *play, off* and *rewind*.

2 *Inductive loop*: The output from the tape recorder is fed into an inductive loop which is plugged into the *output* socket of the tape recorder in place of the extension loudspeaker. The inductive loop is wound on to insulated hooks on a piece of plywood, which is approximately the same size as the table top, and is screwed beneath the table. It is necessary to make the impedance of the loop equal to that of the loudspeaker. In most battery-operated tape recorders this impedance is 8 ohms. At audio frequencies the impedance of the loop is equal to the DC resistance of the wire. Thin enamelled copper wire is satisfactory for this purpose. The length of wire necessary to give the required resistance can easily be calculated from information given in standard wire gauge tables, for example, SWG 28 copper wire has a resistance of .155 ohms per metre. Fifty two metres are required for a resistance of 8 ohms. Having measured the length of wire needed to make one circuit of the plywood ' former ', it is a simple matter to decide the number of ' turns ' to produce the required resistance. When the winding is complete, connection is made to the tape recorder by a length of two core cable and a jack passing through the end of the tape recorder box into the output socket of the tape recorder. This arrangement prevents any unwanted reader interference with the loop or the recorder.

3 *Headset receiver*: Signals from the loop are picked up by a small receiver built into the headphone unit. The wearer can more about freely within the signal area, which, in the example quoted, is within a radius of 12 feet from the loop. Two makes of headset have been used, ' Freelance ' headset manufactured by S G Brown of Watford, England and a much cheaper unit, ' Palca ', of Japanese manufacture.

4 *A book of numbered printed charts*, which includes outline information and annotated sample pages.

This equipment, which is simple and inexpensive, has several limitations. The tape has to be rewound after each session and there is no electronic device which prevents the tape recorder remaining switched ' on ' until the battery is exhausted. The headset receiver is also powered by batteries which may be run down if the switch is left in the 'on' position.

The Massachusetts Institute of Technology have developed a more efficient unit for reader operated tape and chart programs (see plate 6A) which includes the following elements:

1 Mains operated Sony TC40 cassette tape recorder with an endless loop cassette.

2 *Telephone receiver*: Tape recorded instruction is received through a standard telephone receiver. When the hand set is lifted, a mercury switch sets the tape recorder in motion. Once started the program plays to the end, when the tape recorder is automatically switched off and the program is ready for the next listener.

3 *Numbered printed charts,* which are facsimile copies of sample pages on which the relevant information is indicated by coloured patches. The charts are referred to by number in the audio instruction.

TAPE RECORDED INSTRUCTION ILLUSTRATED BY A SYNCHRONISED PROJECTION OF SLIDES

Eastern Michigan University, USA uses a console, designed for their *Audio visual guide to chemical literature,* which is supplied by Gruber Products Co, Toledo, and known as the ' Audio-graph ' (see plate 4B). The unit includes a stereo cassette recorder and a Kodak Carousel projector. The projector is automatically controlled by signals on the tape and the slides are viewed on a screen 24 inches wide and 16 inches high. The tape recordings and slide projection can be reversed independently, but the synchronised automatic control of the slides by the tape is not maintained. The Audio-graph has jack positions for two sets of earphones or a loudspeaker. The relatively large vertical screen makes the equipment suitable for use with individual students and with small groups.

The University of Surrey, England has designed somewhat similar equipment to the Audio-graph described above, which has since been developed by ESL Bristol (see plate 7A). The unit includes a Phillips LCH 1011 cassette recorder having a synchronised control for a Kodak–Type S Carousel projector. The viewing screen measures 10 inches by 7 inches and is almost horizontal. Some care is necessary when loading the carousel magazine, to see that the synchronised control from the tape recorder begins from the correct position, that is to say that the audio program begins with slide one. As with the previously mentioned equipment, once the automatic control sequence has been interrupted, the synchronised control by the tape recorder cannot be brought back into operation except by manual adjustment of the carousel magazine. The equipment, which is available as a single-sided or a double-sided console, has been designed particularly for the SCONUL program, which has already been discussed (chapter 3).

Massachusetts Institute of Technology—Barker library sound slide unit (see plate 7B). This equipment includes a La Belle continuous tape player with synchronised control of the slide projector and a Kodak Carousel AV900 projector fitted with a Buhl 90 degree image shifter. It is mains-powered and housed in a plywood cabinet 20 inches long, 12 inches high and 12 inches deep. On the right is a telephone handset hanging in a cradle, on the left is a viewing screen measuring 6 inches by 5 inches. By lifting the telephone handset from the cradle, the tape recorder is switched on and the program begins. The tape recording is enclosed in an endless loop cassette. When switched on, the audio and slide program continues to the end, when both the tape recorder and the projector are switched off automatically. The program is then ready for use by the next person who lifts the telephone receiver.

MAKING CHARTS

In the context of these notes a chart refers either to printed information which may be on paper or thin card and covering an area about 10 inches by 8 inches, or to a transparency made from such a chart, for use with an overhead projector. The main function of these charts is to supplement and reinforce the information in a live or a recorded lecture, and they fall into three categories:

(*a*) *Outline headings* for the topics covered by a live or a recorded talk, the purpose of which is to emphasise a sequence of ideas and to support audio instruction by visual information.

(*b*) *Library information*, some examples of which are: (i) The layout of a catalogue card and the information on it. (ii) The outline of a classification schedule showing main classes and examples of division and subdivision. (iii) A flow pattern, for example, explaining interloan procedure.

(*c*) *Sample pages* (with explanatory annotations) from documents discussed during a talk.

In preparing charts for categories (*a*) and (*b*), a typewriter may be used, but hand-lettering or transfer lettering is probably more effective. The message should be simple, clear and as brief as possible. It probably helps if the more important ideas are expressed in heavy type or capital letters. The use of a second colour adds interest to a chart and arrests attention. It is often desirable to have more than one copy of a chart. Copying by xerography or one of the other electrostatic processes is most suitable. The copies will, of course, be in black and white, but it is possible to add information in a second colour by hand.

The preparation of charts from sample pages may be a little more complicated. It is seldom practicable to remove pages from a bound book or periodical, so that it is necessary to make a copy of the required page. A dry copying process is most suitable for this purpose, too. If it is desired to add explanatory notes to the page, it may be necessary to add the notes to the xerox copy first, and then to copy the annotated page again. Some definition of the image may be lost in this process, so that it is important that the first copy made from the page in the original document is a good one.

Techniques used in preparing charts depend upon the purposes they are designed to serve, and whether or not they are to be projected on an overhead projector. When projecting the information from a sample page of a document on to a screen, the image is seldom sharp enough for details to be read by a large group. For this reason it is usually necessary to enlarge the information on a representative section of the page. On some charts this enlargement is prepared photographically, but usually a clear enough image can be produced if the representative section of the page is prepared on a typewriter and attached to the sample page. Explanatory annotation can be added in the same way. If it is desired to make a transparency from the modified chart using a heat copying process, it will be necessary to make first a xerograph copy of the chart. Those charts which are designed for individual use may be prepared by ringing significant sections of a page, or by colour-washing as already described.

Physical protection of charts: Charts on paper or card which are likely to be handled frequently can be strengthened and protected by being covered with an adhesive film, such as *transpaseal*. The stiffened charts can be effectively bound together by using a plastic ring binding, which enables each chart to lie flat on a table while being used.

Making transparencies: There are several ways of making transparencies for use on an overhead projector. These may be made on sheets of acetate or melinex film by printing or drawing with a suitable pen. It is important to use the right kind of pen, as characters made with an unsuitable pen, or the wrong kind of ink, may disappear when subjected to heat from the projector lamp. If there is any doubt, a trial chart should be tested on the overhead projector.

The preparation of transparencies by hand is a lengthy process and is not suitable for copying sample pages. There are two simple processes which may be employed. By using specially prepared sheets of film, copies of black and white ' masters ' may be made on xerox electrostatic copiers. One example of this prepared film is 'Arkwright xerographic transparency film '. The other method uses a heat-sensitive film and a master which has the image formed by a deposit of carbon. Lettering in lead pencil or with a typewriter is suitable, but not all hand printed or transfer letters are. Copies of documents made on an electrostatic copier, which uses carbon dust as its printing medium, produce particularly good transparencies. In the heat copying process, the image on the master in carbon conveys heat more quickly than the paper, and thus this image is transferred to the sensitised film. One example of this heat sensitive film is ' 3M infrared transparency film type 135 '.

TAPE RECORDING

These notes are included for librarians who wish to experiment with tape recorded instruction for the first time and who will be using inexpensive equipment and unsophisticated techniques.

Script: The language, scope and amount of detail will depend upon the purpose of the instruction and the people for whom it is prepared. It is probably a good idea first to decide upon a general program, next to select the visual material which will be used to illustrate the talk, and then, to rough out a series of headings before preparing the final script. It may be helpful to record a preliminary talk using only the headings and the visual material. This will give you an idea of the time occupied by the talk, and of the time which should be allowed for viewing the visual elements. By listening to the playback you will be made aware of the quality of reproduction and of the modifications which need to be made. At this point it will be helpful to receive comments from colleagues. From this feedback information, it will be possible to decide on the length of the talk, to make a final selection of visual material and to write a complete script.

The level of recording (*ie* the intensity of the magnetic signals on the tape) depends upon three factors: the power of the recording voice, the distance from the microphone and the degree of amplification applied to the input from the microphone. A workable arrangement is to use a normal speaking voice, to set the level of microphone amplification at about half (in a simple recorder this means setting the volume control at its mid point), and positioning the microphone so that the recording meter or magic eye indicator shows maximum volume without distortion. This arrangement allows for considerable amplification of the recorded voice on playback, if required. Also, there should not be too much distortion. It is important to keep the microphone at a constant distance from the speaker's mouth, and one easy way to achieve this is to hang the microphone around the speaker's neck. This leaves both hands free for holding the script and enables the speaker to sit in a more relaxed position while recording.

More than one voice: It may add interest to recorded instruction to use more than one speaker. When this is done, it is important to keep the level of recording about the same for each voice, which is achieved either by adjusting the position of the microphone or by increasing or decreasing the amount of amplification of the input from the microphone. Almost any kind of microphone can be made to hang from a ribbon tied around the speaker's neck. If the level of recording cannot be adjusted by small changes in amplification then the position of the microphone should be altered.

Tape speed: In a standard reel tape recorder, the tape may travel at several different speeds. Each speed is a multiple of the slowest speed, $1\frac{7}{8}$ inches per second; that is to say, the tape speed can be $1\frac{7}{8}$ inches or $3\frac{3}{4}$ inches, or $7\frac{1}{2}$ inches or 15 inches per second. In principle, a faster tape speed produces a better quality of recording. For practical purposes tape running at $3\frac{3}{4}$ inches per second gives good quality reproduction of speech, and the quality at $1\frac{7}{8}$ inches per second is adequate for instruction programs. The common battery operated cassette recorders have a tape speed of $1\frac{7}{8}$ inches per second.

Background noises are of three kinds:

(*a*) The noises in the building and outside on the roads or in the fields. There is little that can be done in a very noisy environment except to make tape recordings elsewhere. However, some noises are not so intrusive as they seem to be. Microphones are not usually very sensitive to distant noises. A test recording will show how much interference is coming from outside noises.

(*b*) *Loose connections,* particularly in the microphone cable, may cause unpleasant crackling noises. One solution is to sellotape the microphone cord to a chair arm or table leg so that small movements of the microphone do not disturb the plug and socket connection.

(*c*) The crackling of the paper on which the script is written is a particularly common source of unwanted noise. This problem can be eliminated by fastening each sheet of the script to pieces of stiff card with paper clips.

Copying tape recordings: In making instruction tapes for a library, it is helpful to make a master tape on a reel tape recorder at a speed of $3\frac{3}{4}$ inches per second. This is particularly so when more than one voice is used. However, cassette recorders are most convenient for use by students or other library readers, so that it will be necessary to copy the original recording on reel tape on to a cassette. This can be done quite simply by connecting the ' output ' point on reel tape recorder to the ' input ' point on the cassette recorder. Many tape recorders include a lead for this purpose. It is a piece of two-core cable with a jack plug on either end. By setting the playback level on the reel tape recorder to normal speech level, and the recording input level on the cassette recorder to show maximum input without distortion, an accurate copy of the original recording should be made. By a similar arrangement copies can be made from a cassetted master tape by using two cassette tape recorders. In practice, it is helpful to have at least one spare recording available for each program used in the library.

When a large number of copies of a tape recording are required, it may be mentioned that several companies in Britain will copy tape recordings on to cassettes which they supply in quantity at little more than the cost of the empty cassettes. One such firm is Branch and Appleby Ltd of Harrow-on-the-Hill.

No mention has been made of the possibilities of ' editing '. This is essentially a job for experts, and when making a short recording for library instruction, it is simpler and quicker to make a new recording than to attempt to modify the original. It may be worth mentioning, however, that a tape recorder speed may vary slightly from the standard speed, so that its recordings may play back satisfactorily only on the recording machine. That is to say, the recording could not be played without distortion on a second machine. This problem can be overcome by copying the original recording on to a tape on the second machine.

concept of self-service is a common one in our society. The services needed by readers in a library are often as simple and straight-forward as those provided by the commercial services and, when this is the case, much of the service can be given more effectively and economically by self-service methods. The other proposition is that an element of exploitation can be assumed to be a necessary part of a wide range of library activity. Let us consider a few examples:

1 A library decides to make a change in the *loans procedure*. The exploitation element is represented by the *publicity* which prepares readers in advance for the change, and by adequate *explanation* of the new technique during the first few weeks after the change takes place. This publicity and explanation may take several forms, and the combination of a *news board* and short-term hand-outs for such purposes has already been discussed.

2 A library decides to set up a *microfilm reader* for its library users. The exploitation element is represented by an adequate, easily-read set of *instructions* telling people how to put film or fiche on the reader; how to operate the machinery; how to focus the image on the screen and whether there are any extra facilities, such as the ability to print off individual frames or sections of the text.

3 A *new periodical* is purchased by a library. The exploitation elements would include the setting up of a clearly readable *shelf label*, and possibly an addition to the *list of new periodicals received*.

4 A catalogue is prepared for the library. The exploitation activity would include clear, easily-read drawer *labels*, regular *guide cards* in the catalogue drawers, and a panel describing what each part of the catalogue records, the principles behind the classification scheme, *and instructions* for using the cata-logue.

The first example was largely a *public relations* exercise. The second example dealt simply with a library service which was made more accessible by being made easy to use. There is nothing complicated about using a microfilm reader when there is simple information about the controls and directions how to use them.

In the third example, readers using the periodicals area of the library are made aware of the position of the new periodical; and, from another point of view, by using the supplement to the *periodicals list,* readers become aware of the new periodical as an addition to the library stock. The fourth example indicates how a library catalogue may be transformed from a mysterious device, exclusively for the use of librarians, to an accessible aid which can be simply used by any reader.

EXPLOITATION DEPARTMENT

Few librarians would consider taking into library stock a work of non-fiction or serious fiction without recording it in a catalogue. This recording process may well represent a higher sum in staff time and overhead expenses than the original price paid for the book to the bookseller. However, little corresponding effort is expended in ' directing the flow ' of books to the reader—in the words of Ranganathan, in seeing that the book reaches its reader, that the reader finds the required book, and also that he is saved wasted time when he is doing so. It is, perhaps, as important to have the library stock used as it is to record items in a catalogue. Exploitation activity extends into every department of a library, and therefore the function of an exploitation section or department is primarily to co-ordinate activities which have their origin in the various departments of the library. Also, since exploitation in this sense is not widely understood by library staff, a large amount of effort is required to train and accustom the staff to the change in approach to library service. Since the library changes and grows all the time, exploitation activity is continually evolving.

In order to establish and maintain a system of exploitation in the library, some redirection of staff time and effort is required. Although a wide range of exploitation techniques has been discussed, piecemeal, it may be helpful to summarise the responsibilities of a separate section of a library with the overall function of co-ordinating all exploitation devices and services.

1 To design and develop an exploitation program which will suit the requirements of the individual library, as a broad concept, including guiding, publication and personal service to readers.

2 To design the various elements of a self-service guiding scheme, permanent visual information, colour-coding, and audio visual aids.

3 To select the materials and equipment necessary to give effect to a self-service guiding scheme. This selection would include the materials for the panels and signs; also, the frames, stands and other fittings which may be required. Tape recorders, projectors and similar teaching aids would be included, too.

4 To produce the necessary items of library literature, including tape recording scripts, printed guides, and information leaflets.

5 To arrange publicity especially for changes in, or additions to, the service to readers, by notices on a *news board* and by distribution of printed leaflets.

6 To co-ordinate all aspects of the service to readers by library staff, through the establishment of an agreed program for such activities as the readers' adviser services; library instruction classes for students in college and universities; and, liaison between the library staff and teachers in teaching institutions of all kinds.

7 To establish measures to give library staff at every level an understanding of the working of all aspects of the exploitation program. The systems approach is designed to save time for library users, including people on the staff of the library who use the resources of the library most widely.

8 To maintain all parts of the exploitation program in good working order.

(*a*) To keep a watching brief over the re-shelving of books and their arrangement in the shelves in correct classified order.

(*b*) To make sure that the positioning of shelf labels is correct and relevant.

(*c*) To ensure that new shelf labels are set up as necessary.

(*d*) To ensure that minor changes in the location of library stock are indicated by appropriate signs or labels.

(*e*) To arrange for the up-dating of permanent visual information when major changes in library organisation make this desirable.

(*f*) To arrange for the up-dating of information in printed guides by adding supplements or by preparing a new edition when required. To watch that leaflets and more ephemeral library publications have a purpose and are relevant, and to remove or replace those which are obsolete.

(*g*) To arrange for regular maintenance and servicing of tape recorders and other equipment.

(*h*) To keep watch on ordering routines for special collections to guard against the development of gaps in government publications, report series, etc.

(*i*) To make sure that the information transmitted through reader-operated audio visual aids is relevant and in line with the most recent developments. For example, the facilities offered by some of the major abstracting services have changed considerably in recent years. Such changes may make major modifications necessary in the audio and the visual elements of 'automatic' information. It is likely too that readers will have more confidence in 'automatic' information if the sample pages cited are from recent issues of a publication.

STAFFING

In addition to the responsibilities for the design and maintenance of the system, the staff of the section will need to include someone with practical skills, preferably with the ability to produce the necessary labels and signs, to make simple fittings and to maintain audio visual aids.

It would also be a helpful principle if people from other library departments could serve for short periods in the exploitation section. Since there is an exploitation aspect to every library activity, the more widely the ramifications of the program are understood by library staff, the more effective the system will become.

154

Exploitation techniques apply in all libraries. That is to say, all librarians want to see people read the books which are in their charge.

However, a system of exploitation has a particular application in the libraries of places where people teach. The function of libraries in such organisations is to contribute to the teaching and learning program, and the more closely the library activity is integrated into the teaching and learning arrangements, the more effective is its role.

Having said that, for the working of the exploitation system to be successful it is necessary for it first to be recognised as an integral part of the library policy by the librarian and his staff and by the institution as a whole. Such acceptance recognises certain changes of emphasis in library service. One criticism of a self-service scheme of any kind is that it permits the service staff to have an easier time, or cuts down the number of service staff needed. In a library, the purpose is rather to sift out the routine information which can be supplied to readers, as well, or better, on a self-service basis, so that the time of the library can be occupied in giving personal assistance to readers of a more worth-while kind. Self-service information also has the advantage of being available to readers at all times, whether the library staff are busy or not. By co-ordinating exploitation activity, individual members of the library staff are more aware of what the library is trying to do. For example, when there is an agreed program for liaison with the teaching staff, each member of staff concerned with this work will know what the library objectives are and how his or her efforts fit into the general scheme. More time and energy will be expended in preparing aids and supervising routines than in answering miscellaneous queries from readers, often at an elementary level. By reference to these aids, very many more members of library staff are able to help readers in finding information. By means of these aids, too, newly joined members of the library staff may quickly appreciate the services offered by the library and how the readers may best make use of them.

It would be unreasonable to suggest that the services to readers which have been mentioned in this section are not already provided effectively in a great number of libraries at the present time. What perhaps is new in this approach to exploitation is that these services should be co-ordinated under a general plan of action. The other concept which may also be new is that an exploitation element should be regarded as a necessary part of all library activity. It is commonly-accepted practice in libraries that when a book is purchased it is automatically recorded in the catalogue, which is of course the beginning of the exploitation program. However, it is not so widely accepted that, when there is a catalogue, it is also necessary to set up clear instructions so that all the readers can use it.

An exploitation program or system such as has been described in this manual represents some departure from established practice. In the early stages of the introduction of such a scheme, a good deal of tact is necessary, even when the project has received official blessing. Each library is individual; and, to some librarians, one aspect of exploitation will appeal more than another. Also, of course, the needs of one library differ from those of another.

In establishing a system in a library there are two general guidelines. The first is to make the maximum use of all existing exploitation aids, labels, signs, guides and library literature, so that as much as possible of the accepted and familiar is incorporated into the program. The second is to allow time for unfamiliar ideas to sink in and to become significant. For example, one college library held a full set of titles for the periodicals shelves unused for twelve months. It was not until changes in staff indicated the great waste of time taking place during routine shelving of these publications, that the value of the shelf labels was realised.

Many similar examples could be cited.

8

Some recent developments

THE DEVELOPMENTS WHICH HAVE affected the ease with which library resources may be exploited have taken place in three areas:

1 The several automatic instruction programs which have been designed to show readers how to use libraries and information.

2 The use of document copying techniques.

3 The application of the computer for storing and retrieving information.

AUTOMATIC INSTRUCTION

This topic has already been discussed in some detail, and several examples of audio and audio-visual programs have been examined. The applications of these teaching aids have gone beyond the experimental stage, and there is likely to be a great increase in their use as soon as inexpensive hardware becomes commercially available. The experiments at Massachusetts Institute of Technology have resulted in a compact and robust playback unit which has overcome two common difficulties for libraries, the problem of automatically switching off the power supply after use, and the automatic resetting of the program so that the tape recording is ready to begin when required by the next listener.

The most widely used audio visual programs for library exploitation employ tape recordings illustrated by slides or charts and emphasis is still being placed upon these combinations. Librarians have long been familiar with the films and filmstrips which are available, but there is increasing use now being made of videotape recordings and closed circuit television. When the necessary equipment and expertise is available, a videotape program can be inexpensively set up; and many such programs have been described in the literature.

Tape/chart and tape/slide programs have very many applications. For groups, they may take the place of lectures, especially when used to stimulate enquiry, as for instance in the *Information officer project* (chapter 9), where the information officers prepared audio visual information programs of several different kinds, and displayed them to groups of students in order to stimulate enquiry as a preparation for individual literature searches.

There are obvious advantages in using tapes and slides in this way. There is much greater opportunity for careful preparation, and there is the saving for the instructor of handing on repetitive information. These aids may also be used by teachers and instructors of various kinds as a basis for personal instruction; either to groups or to individuals. Finally, the widest use of these aids is as a program for instructing individual library readers, especially in the use of bibliographic aids and the catalogue.

Videotape and closed circuit television can be used in a similar way, although both these media have been less extensively tested in the context of library exploitation. Television techniques have qualities of immediacy and an intimate relationship with the viewer which may be important. Physically, videotape is a more compact form of storage for audio visual material, especially when cassetted videotape becomes more common. Videotape recording has many of the advantages of cine-photography. Movement and continuous activity can be portrayed, and sound effects and spoken language can be naturally integrated with the visual information. Preparation of a program is comparatively simple and ' playback ' is possible at any stage during preparation. When the program is complete, the record is completely portable and the tapes may be copied electronically, if it is desired to use the program in several different places at the same time. The size of group is limited to the number able to view a single television screen. However, the author has had experience of one university where, in a large lecture room, the television output is connected to a dozen television receivers sited so that all the viewers can clearly see at least one screen.

Some document copying techniques have been briefly discussed. There are two broad types of photocopying, full size copying and micro copying.

As an exploitation device, full size or ' readable size ' copying has affected the availability of information very considerably, especially in the supply of out of print materials. This has had a particular importance in overseas libraries which have now been able to obtain copies of a number of older standard works and the back issues of periodicals. The rapid document copying techniques by electrostatic processes such as xerography have been particularly significant in this field. Most librarians are familiar with the catalogues of the British Museum, which have in recent years been produced by a similar technique. The reduced print size, achieved photographically, has resulted in a great saving of space and paper. The photocopying of book sections and periodical articles for interloan purposes has three advantages:

1 The original document does not leave the parent library and need not be away from the shelves for more than a short time.

2 There is a considerable saving in postage and in packing time.

3 The photocopied text may remain with the borrower for as long as it is needed.

These factors have not only increased the availability of information to readers; the fact that the parent library is able to keep its books has removed much of the justifiable reluctance to lend to other libraries.

MICROFORMS

Most librarians are familiar with some microform library resources; but it may be helpful to define a few of the terms used and to look at some of the types of microtexts.

By the term *microform* or *microtext* we simply mean reduced photographic copies of documents. Each exposure, which may be of one or two pages of the original document, is known as a frame. There are two common *microforms : microfilm* is roll film, which is usually 16 or 35 millimetres in width, in which the frames are arranged singly along the length of the film. *Microfiche* is sheet film, with various surface sizes (commonly A6 paper size) and in which the frames are arranged horizontally. There are several ways that roll film may be converted to fiches. One way is to use transparent *jackets,* within which there are slots into which strips of roll film can be inserted. A second way is to stick strips of film to a transparent base.

Microfiches may be stored vertically in drawers and arranged in any required sequence. The aperture card is a special development of this technique, in which an opaque card has an aperture into which a strip of microfilm can be inserted. One important application is for the storage and retrieval of engineering drawings in a large drawing office. The drawings are photographed on to 70 millimetre film and inserted into the aperture of a tabulator card which can be mechanically retrieved. As required, full sized blue prints can be made photographically from the microfilm image.

Microcards are microtexts on opaque glossy cards; a common size is 5 inches by 3 inches. These are not now very commonly used as the image when displayed on a screen is not so clear as from a transparency.

There are several different forms of microfiche and each is usually described by an accepted term. The term *microfiche* refers usually to micro copies with a reduction ratio of $^1/_{16}$ to $^1/_{24}$ of the original. One microfiche of the A6 size could contain about seventy pages. For the next degree of reduction the term *superfiche* is used. The reduction ratio is about $1/_{50}$ to $^1/_{100}$ of the original. A common size is 5 inches by 3 inches and a superfiche contains about 1,000 pages. The highest reduction ratio produces what is known as an *ultrafiche,* in which the image is about $^1/_{100}$ to $^1/_{200}$ of the original, and an ultrafiche measuring 6 inches by 4 inches could contain 3,000 pages.

As an element in exploitation, microforms are extremely important. We have already discussed some of the advantages of full size copying. Microforms have all the same advantages with the added ones that microfilm or microfiche is cheaper to produce or to copy, and is very much more easily portable. A long book can be contained on a comparatively small roll of film, or, in fact, on a single superfiche. Microfilm is permanent and durable, the surface scratches have very little effect on the readability of the enlarged image, and microfiche or jacketed microfilm can be stored vertically and arranged into any convenient order. In the library, information stored on microtexts can save a great deal of space and weight. For instance, 100 standard microfiches, with a reduction ratio of $^1/_{10}$ to $^1/_{20}$ of the original text, each containing sixty to seventy pages, could hold the standard texts for a university course. A brief description of an experimental course using microtexts in this way is given below.

DISADVANTAGES

There are some disavantages in using microtexts. First of all, the average library user prefers to read conventional books; also, some eye strain may be caused by reading the projected image on a lighted screen; and, of course, an optical device for enlarging the microtext and for projecting it on to a screen is necessary. Lastly, the images may fade in strong light when the film is not prepared for special archival purposes.

Microfilm readers of various kinds are available in all the larger libraries. In general, the higher reduction material such as *superfiche* and *ultrafiche* require more expensive reading machines. As an aid towards better exploitation of microtext resources, a large number of readers have a *printout* facility, that is to say, the frames containing the information which is required by the reader for permanent reference may be copied in readable size photographically. Thus, if a reader needs an article from a periodical stored on microfilm, readable copy is easily available. This type of copy can be expensive, particularly when the copying facility is little used. Many of the copiers still use a wet copying system with a developing fluid which quickly deteriorates with keeping. However, there are now one or two readers with dry copying capabilities which may overcome this difficulty, although the capital cost is high.

EXPERIMENTAL UNIVERSITY COURSE USING STANDARD TEXTS ON MICROFICHES[1]

In 1971, the University of South Africa had a student population of 25,000, most of whom received courses by correspondence. Because of the difficulty which students experienced in obtaining the set books, it was decided to supply some titles on microfiches. 110 texts were selected for the experiment. From the beginning it was realised that some objections might be raised by the publishers, and it was proposed by the university that the publishers should be paid ten per cent of the published price for each book reproduced on microfiches. There were some reservations, but most of the publishers agreed to this arrangement. Thirty DASA readers were purchased, many of which were sent to individual students by post. There were difficulties: postal despatch was not ideal, the reader lamps did not last as long as was expected, and some students complained of eye strain. However, for one experimental group of third year library students, it was found that twice the average number of titles was borrowed and four times as many students used the library.

COMPUTER APPLICATIONS

The literature of librarianship now abounds with examples of the applications of computers in libraries, for the storage and retrieval of information and also for administrative routines.

As an exploitation device, the computer is mainly useful in two ways: first of all, in the widened and time-saving aspects of information storage and retrieval; and, secondly, as a means of recording random information which can be reproduced in an ordered fashion, particularly in the compilation of catalogues; but, in this connection, the most important recent development is the utilisation of microfilm as the medium for direct computer printout. In information storage the computer, of course, is able to record the details of basic information, for example the details of a periodical article, and this information may be retrieved automatically under various headings—authors, subjects, the name of the periodical, and so on.

There are five stages in this process. In the first place, the information must be put into the computer; and it is at this point that the human element is a decisive factor. The input to a computer is usually in the form of punched card, punched paper tape or magnetic tape. When the input has been prepared, the information on it is stored in the computer. This store may be an integral part of the computer's electronic memory or on removeable magnetic tapes or discs.

In principle, there is no limit to the amount of detail which can be put into a computer store, but in practice, for an information service, the amount of detail will be limited to the most significant items. For a report or a periodical article, this would include full bibliographical detail plus a few extra key words or *descriptors,* which will add to the information supplied by the title. Some services also record abstracts.

The next stage is that retrieval instructions must be drawn up. That is to say, a program must be compiled so that the information can be retrieved under the required headings or in the desired sequences.

Finally, an output must be produced in some humanly readable form. This may be a printout on paper, a cathode ray tube display, or a microfilm. It is of interest to note that the printout stage can be the most time-consuming and, therefore, may be the most expensive.

There are now a very large number of computer or *machine* information storage and retrieval services in Britain, and there are very many more such services offered in the United States. Also, a great number of large companies and government departments operate internal machine information storage and retrieval systems. Many of these machine services have developed from standard printed abstracting and indexing services.

A few examples of commercial sources are described below. For a long time now computers have been used to speed up the production of abstracting services and to compile a range of indexes which would otherwise not have been economically justified. Perhaps the commonest indication of the activity of the computer is the large number of *keyword indexes* which have been published in the past ten years, by such well known abstracting services as *Chemical abstracts* and *Biological abstracts*.

In the keyword index the title is printed several times, once for each important word in the title. The significant words are then arranged by the computer in columns in alphabetical order. Librarians are all familiar with these keyword indexes and the limitations imposed by line length.

As an extension of the keyword index service, machine retrieval services offer to retrieve information for specific researchers, and to do this they have asked their clients to supply a list of terms under which information should be retrieved. These lists of words or terms follow a technique somewhat like a keyword index. Basically, the terms are in four categories.

1 The authors in whose work the researcher is interested.

2 The keywords under which the researcher expects to find the required information.

3 The journals in which the researcher expects to find useful information.

4 The combinations of authors, journals and keywords which will limit the amount of *noise,* or irrelevant information, which is retrieved. In the MIT audio guide for *Science citation index,* one combination of terms was ' Mossbauer ' and ' effect '. Here is an example of two terms being used together for a search, and this is the kind of information which might be included in a profile.

COMPUTER OUTPUT ON MICROFILM

This combines the flexibility of computer storage and retrieval with a rapid readable output. There are very many advantages to this form of output.

First of all, the speed of printout is up to 30 times faster than mechanical printout on paper (about one thousand pages per hour). Within the library, the computer printout on microfilm for a catalogue provides a great saving of space; for example, the details of the books added to a large public library in one year could be recorded in a single cassette of sixteen millimetre film. Lastly, a cassette microfilm reader replaces several cabinets of catalogue drawers. Also, the reader display restores the convenience of the printed catalogue form, in that a page of entries can be viewed at a glance and the catalogue user can obtain all the information in it without moving from the display screen.

From the point of view of exploitation, when the copying of records is particularly important, multiple copies of a microfilm catalogue can be made very quickly and very cheaply. For example, in Britain, the present cost of a duplicate cassette of diazo roll film with a capacity of 15-20,000 entries would be approximately £2. It is, of course, necessary to add to this figure the cost of installing one or more microfilm readers at each catalogue point in the library. The present cost of a cassette reader is from £50-100. Therefore, in a large library, complete copies of the catalogue could be made available in several places at a very small cost once the master catalogue has been recorded on a computer. COM (computer on microfilm) catalogues are used in Britain by Westminster Public Libraries in London, by county libraries in Flintshire and Cornwall, and by Birmingham University Library. At these libraries, the microfilm catalogues have been well received by the readers.

MICRO PUBLISHING

Publication in the form of microfilm or michofiche is well established in research organisations such as NASA, and in government departments. This represents a particularly cheap way of disseminating information for small groups of people where commercial and profit motives do not require consideration. Some journals are also now issuing hard copies with parallel microform versions. J H Kuney[4] suggests a system of publication with a printed journal which would publish digests of papers with the full texts published as a microfiche. However, it may be worth mentioning two publications of special interest to librarians.

Books in English lists the books published in Britain, USA, Canada, Australia, etc and is published by the British National

Bibliography in collaboration with the US Library of Congress. This information is prepared from the tapes of MARC (machine readable catalogue) compiled in Britain and the USA, and produced as ultrafiche by the National Cash Register Co. Each ultrafiche contains about three thousand pages, and the bibliography is published in this form, at present every two months. The National Cash Register Co also supplies the high magnification ultrafiche readers necessary to use *Books in English*. MARC tapes have already had a brief mention when discussing the film ' SBN 72 ' (chapter 3). The National Cash Register Co is re-publishing on *ultrafiche* several thousand volumes of standard works with the general theme, 'American civilization '.

Encyclopaedia Britannica (USA) is also republishing a similar series on *superfiche* (one book on each superfiche). The republishing of standard works as microforms is likely to increase, so that it may be possible in the future to send a standard work to any library in the world for the cost of posting a letter.

SOME EXAMPLES OF MACHINE RETRIEVAL SYSTEMS[2]
There are four kinds of service offered by machine retrieval services:

1 Retrospective searching to supplement or take the place of a hand search.

2 SDI (selective dissemination of information) or current awareness services which are based upon similar individual profile information. The computer searches the current literature, that is to say, the information in the new tapes as they are compiled. The user of the service is informed of the current papers, say, every two weeks. This service is designed to take the place of regular reading by research people of their literature and the abstracts.

3 Standard profile services covering several hundred topics. Subjects on which a great number of people require information are regularly searched, and the results of these searches may be purchased at a much cheaper rate than the information obtained for individual research requirements.

4 Owners of these services will hire or lease complete tapes or

files of information, recorded in their computer systems, for processing on the hirer's own computer. Many of the services in Britain are based upon material of this kind leased from American sources.

COMPUTERISED INFORMATION SERVICES

1 BA *Previews* (USA) is based upon information in *Biological abstracts,* and includes full bibliographical detail but without an abstract. The services offered include *standard profiles, recurring bibliography,* and *retrospective searches.* The information is being disseminated in Britain by arrangement with the American originators, who send the magnetic tape to Britain for processing.

2 *Psychological abstracts* (USA). Three-monthly computer tapes containing bibliographic detail and abstracts may be leased, and individual searches can be carried out.

3 *INSPEC Tape Services* (Information services in physics, electrotechnology, computers and control)—Institution of Electrical Engineers, London, England. Tapes with and without abstracts in three subject areas, *physics, electronics, computers and control, are* available for leasing. A regular weekly SDI service, based upon individual searcher's profiles, is also offered. Each reference is printed out on to individual 6 × 4 inch cards. A *standard profile* service on a very large number of topics is also available.

4 MEDLARS (medical literature analysis retrieval system) is based upon information in *Index medicus*—approximately one million articles from 3,000 journals. Search terms are rigidly controlled in a list known as MESH (Medical subject headings). This is the most widely used machine retrieval service in Britain. Tapes from America are processed at Newcastle University, and the service in Britain is controlled from the National Lending Library for Science and Technology at Boston Spa.

COST OF COMPUTER SEARCHING

In a short manual of this kind it would not be helpful to give examples of costs of computer information retrieval, which vary a great deal from one service to another, and which are based upon complicated calculations. It will be noted, however, that in the *Information officer project* the cheapest form of current awareness service, at a cost of about £40-80 a year, was not widely used by academic research people, on the grounds of cost, although some individual machine searches were considered to be good value.

DIRECT ACCESS TO COMPUTERISED INFORMATION

The most recent development in computer information services provides for facilities to search a central computer store from distant points. At each distant point there will also be equipment to produce a readable output. These services are not at present generally available in libraries in Britain; but over the next five years, an extensive experimental project in five scientific and academic libraries is being sponsored by OSTI. The proposed experiments will be based upon the computer files for *Science citation index* and *Computer abstracts* as a data source, and upon the Post Office telephone lines as a means of communication.

REFERENCES

1 John Willemse: ' Preliminary report on an experimental project to supply recommended books to students in microfiche form ', *NRCd bulletin* Summer 1972 5 (3) 69-72.

2 Ruth Finer: *A guide to selected computer based information services.* Aslib, 1972.

3 B J S Williams: *Microform applications in library catalogues: report to the ADP Project.* National Reprographic Centre for Documentation, 1972.

4 J H Kuney: ' The role of microfilms in journal publication ', *Journal of chemical documentation 12* (2) 1972 79-80.

9

Experiments in methods of exploitation

COMPARATIVELY LITTLE WORK has been done by libraries to find out how their resources are being used, what factors influence readers in the use of information, and what criteria can be established to measure the effectiveness of library use. Most of the work that has been done in this field has taken place in college and university libraries. Although there has been a large number of readership surveys, especially in university libraries, these surveys are designed to find out information about readers, how and why and where they use libraries and for what purpose. Such surveys give little indication of how well the resources of the library are being exploited, that is, how much or how thoroughly the books and information services are being used, whether some sections of the resources are very heavily used, whether some are neglected altogether, and why this should happen.

As has already been mentioned, the main effort exerted by the libraries of colleges and universities to exploit more fully the use of their resources has been to provide some form of library instruction. For this reason it will be of interest to examine the Monteith project, which has already been briefly mentioned. Two other lines of investigation have made a significant contribution in the general field of library exploitation research, the 'University information officer' project sponsored by the Office for Scientific and Technical Information at the Department of Education and Science in Britain, and the 'Readers shelf failure' surveys made by the Library Management Research Unit of Cambridge University Library in Britain. Finally there are some notes on student library use at Hatfield Polytechnic.

MONTEITH PROJECT[1]
This was carried out at Monteith College of the Wayne State

University between 1960 and 1962, under the auspices of US Office of Education, Dept of Health and Welfare. Quoting from the final report on the project:

' The proposal for the study (that is, the application to US Office of Education) cited evidence in research literature to support the contention that " traditional college instruction fails to exploit fully the library resources available for it, and, that the average college student's experience with the library constitutes a limited and fairly insignificant part of his education ". We felt that this was a problem of special concern at the present time because of the " current emphasis upon independent study . . . since it is certainly reasonable to assume that a capacity for independent study implies competence in the use of books and other library resources. The objectives of the project are stated as follows:

' " The ultimate purpose of the Monteith Library program is to stimulate and guide students in developing a sophisticated understanding of the library and increasing competence in its use. To achieve this end, it proposes to provide students with experiences which are functionally related to their course work. Planning such experiences will involve library instructional co-ordination on an unprecedented scale. . . ." '

Monteith College was then a small, new college (established 1959) in a very large university. Its purpose was to provide a general liberal education in three departments, *science of society*, *natural sciences* and *humanities*. The number of students during the project period rose from 300 to 700, and the academic staff from 15 to 30. The undergraduate course lasted four years, and was organised to give the student an increasing responsibility for directing his own efforts of study. The concept of the college was an experimental one, and the setting could be regarded as particularly favourable for library research. Professor Knapp already had research experience and had carried out a somewhat similar investigation at Knox College, Illinois.[2]

The research project was carried out in two phases—a short preliminary period, which provided information to make effective the longer and more complete second phase. From the beginning it was recognised that library teaching could only be effective if it had the co-operation and active support of the academic staff, and further, that any practical work should be part of the complete teaching program. Special support for the project came from the Head of the Science of Society Department and from the Chief Librarian of the University Main Library, where all the practical work was carried out.

The project staff comprised the following people: The project director, who was responsible for the general administration of the project; the project librarian; a research analyst, who was a sociologist and responsible for gathering and analysing the statistical results of the experiment; one research assistant; twenty five bibliographic assistants (students—mostly graduates), who worked part time for 10 hours per week. Later the number was reduced to 14 students each working 15 hours per week.

The first phase of the project had three objectives:

1 To set the students four test assignments which were presented to them by the teachers, and which were accompanied by very full notes written by the project librarian.

2 To analyse the institutional problems involved, that is, to see how academic staff used the library; to examine their attitudes towards library personnel, and their general evaluation of the library in the teaching program. The information was obtained partly by interviews and partly from discussions with the bibliographic assistants, whose main function was to assist the academic staff with their library needs.

3 A random sample of 21 students was paid to spend two days in the library in order to make a detailed analysis of their library behaviour. They were given a series of specially prepared library performance tests and certain capability tests. They also completed a questionnaire giving details of their background and of their experiences with the library program.

Phase two of the project was concerned with the results of a more extended series of library assignments, which were presented to students with accompanying notes, and were preceded by periods of discussion with the project staff.

The term 'products' rather than 'results' was chosen in the original report. In discussing the *institutional problems*, the first point that was made was that the organisation of a library is 'vertical' and control is 'hierarchial', while the organisation of academic staff is largely horizontal in that individual teachers can make decisions as to the content of courses and the method of teaching. The second comment was that although the project staff were accepted by the academic staff as colleagues, they were never regarded as part of the teaching team.

The academic staff all used the library for the preparation of lectures and reading lists; but it was pointed out that, in this college, most of the courses were new and the lectures were being prepared for the first time.

Student reactions: The project included 14 assignments, and from the resulting work by students and the reactions of the teaching staff, three aspects of the problems involved were highlighted:

1 For an assignment to be closely related to the students' course work was not enough. Students' motives for using the library derived from the value placed upon such work by the course instructor.

2 The systems of scholarly reporting and the systems of library organisation are not identical, and this difference is important in designing a course of library instruction; that is, the structure of a literature must be taught.

3 Finally, the concept of a sophisticated understanding of the library and increasing competence in its use as a goal of general education is not accepted, perhaps not understood [by either students or by teachers].

Assessment of results of the experiment: Much effort was expended to record the results of all aspects of the experiments, and one of the project staff had this special responsibility. There were three general conclusions:

1 Measuring or assessing higher levels of competence in library use is difficult if not impossible.

2 If the needs of the teaching program include a wide use of

library resources, the library was used extensively; otherwise, students made little use of information in the library, except that for required reading.

3 No useful correlation existed between the marks awarded to students for their library assignments and those received in the final examinations.

THE OSTI PROJECT: INFORMATION OFFICERS IN UNIVERSITY LIBRARIES[3]

This project ran from January 1970 to December 1972. Six information officers were appointed to six universities in Britain, which were selected to give a coverage of old and new universities in widely separated areas of the country. The duties of information officers were described in the following terms:

' It is envisaged that the information officer would be responsible for education and training of academic staff and postgraduate students in the use of information resources. While not directly concerned with introductory courses for undergraduates on library use, he would give such assistance as he could to other library staff running such courses. He would also promote effective use of information services both traditional and mechanised; and, these objectives would be met through formal courses, or seminars, and through advice and assistance with individual information problems. Information officers would not be expected to perform routine library tasks, and some clerical assistance would be provided; also, a small sum of money would be allowed for bibliographic or other aids.'

In each university a project committee was set up comprising the university librarian as project head, the information officer and representatives from osti. The information officers met several times during the project period in order to pool their experiences, and to discuss problems which had arisen at each university. Otherwise, each information officer arranged a program to suit the special circumstances at the university to which he was appointed. The project was aimed mainly at postgraduates, the academic staff and people doing research. These people could be expected to need information in depth and to make a wide use of library resources. *The exploitation techniques* used included all the well established methods of exploiting library resources:

1 Helping individuals with information problems at all levels.

2 Since the project had as one purpose, that of explaining and publicising machine retrieval services, assistance with the preparation of profiles was an important part of this work.

3 Holding seminars, usually for 8-12 people with information needs in a similar subject area, for example, management students, seeking sources of statistical information.

4 Giving more formal lectures to large groups.

5 Publishing subject guides and other library literature.

6 Preparation of sound/slide programs, videotapes and similar aids.

7 Liaison with professors, tutors and other teaching staff.

For the purpose of these notes the universities concerned are identified by the letters 'A-F'. A full report of the experiment will be published in 1974 as an Aslib *Occasional paper*.

'A' was an old established university with a population of about 3,000 undergraduates and 700 postgraduates. The library facilities included a main library and several self-contained departmental and sectional libraries, some of which were a mile distant from the main library. These distances made the work of the information officer more difficult. A further difficulty was the need to control too great a demand for interloan requests because of the extra work load for the library staff. Some ' institutional ' problems were similar to those experienced at Monteith. In such a large population, the information officer could only make contact with a tiny proportion of the staff and students, but some 60 individuals were introduced to mechanised retrieval services, the most popular being MEDLARS. 25 items of library literature were prepared, the demand for several items of which increased each year.

Seminars and lectures, which were always supported by handouts, usually lasted about an hour. Some groups received three or four lectures, and during the experiment, students and academic staff from 25 departments attended these sessions. About half the lectures were for second or third year undergraduates.

The demand for lectures and seminars increased with each year of the experimental period.

' B ' was an old established provincial university with a population of about 8,000, described as being large, well organised, apathetic, inflexible and uncommunicative. The library facilities again included several self-contained departmental libraries. One initial problem was the difficulty of making so large an academic staff aware of the existence of an information officer.

No lectures or seminars were given in the first year; and 39 during the whole period. Departments representing about $^1/_5$ of the university population were contacted, and 70 computer searches were organised. Feedback information was carefully analysed by following up lectures and computer searches by circular letters. Response was graded as ' enthusiastic ', ' very interested ', ' interested ' and ' disinterested '. About half the people who received lectures asked for them to be repeated in the next year.

Two comments by the information officer are of particular interest. One referred to difficulties in retrieving information because of the organisation of reference materials and the other to the difficulty which readers experience in finding specific items in the library. Together with this comment was the remark that the library's holdings of primary material was more than adequate.

' C ' was one of the new universities, originally a college of advanced technology. The attitude of people using information was somewhat different from that obtaining in the older established universities. Before the experiment began, a well developed library service was provided. A number of computer retrieval schemes were in operation, photocopying was free for staff and postgraduates, and interlibrary loan was unlimited. Adequate printed guides were in use and the library was organised into broad subject departments. During the first year of the experiment the information officer's task was made more difficult because of the overcrowding in the library and the move to new library premises. The majority of lectures were to postgraduate groups, and lasted about an hour. The lecture information was supported by printed handouts. The library had good collections of bibliographic airs and there was, a few miles away, another very large university library.

At this university, the work of the information officer received active acceptance, and the librarian reported that the stage had been reached when serious consideration was being given to the embodiment of an information requirement in degree courses.

' D ' was a university established in the last century with a strong bias towards the sciences.

The library facilities were served by a medium-sized main library and about 15 largish departmental libraries. The policy of the institution did not favour centralisation. There is also a large scientific library in the vicinity, which, although not part of the university, may be used by its students and academic staff.

About 50 lectures or seminars were arranged, mostly for post-graduates. Some 15 guides and handouts were prepared, which were used as supporting literature for seminars and for subject displays in the library. Also a forty-minute videotape program, introducing the catalogue, some reference works and a selection of bibliographic aids, was prepared by the information officer and one of the lecturers, using a question and answer technique. During the project period 18 machine searches were organised.

' E ' is another of the new universities which had already experimented with library introduction techniques. Seminars were offered to third and fourth year undergraduates and to post-graduates.

A series of up to date guides was in use, and preference was given to the purchase of bibliographic aids rather than to long runs of periodicals. There was a limit of two interloans per week for undergraduates, although postgraduates were able to obtain as many outside loans as they needed. A number of machine retrieval services were also in use. The library had a closely integrated exploitation program, a system of updating for library literature, and there was close co-operation between readers, advisers and information officer. 36 lectures were given in the first year of the experiment, and 141 during the project. A particular feature of the program was the series of lectures on thesis-presentation in the first year.

' F ' was a large, new university with a special interest in advanced interdisciplinary teaching, involving a large amount of independent study and a heavy use of the library as a consequence. User-instruction was given to several groups of undergraduates and post-graduates. The subject enquiries were handled by a *Readers advisory group,* which contained a number of subject specialists. Sub-librarians had regular contacts with academic liaison representatives. During the first year, the information officer requested the purchase of a number of abstracting journals considered necessary for postgraduate literature searching. In the university, emphasis was placed upon the needs of undergraduates, and consequently the journal holdings of the library were not large and increase in literature searching by postgraduates would increase the already very heavy load on the library interloan department. A further problem was the filing of bibliographic aids in several different sections of the library.

After the first year the majority of the lectures was offered to undergraduates, mostly to students of the applied sciences. Three tape/slide programs were prepared, each of which illustrated a model search on a specific topic; and 28 machine searches were organised.

At each stage in the project, the information officer had to guard against creating a demand which could not be handled by the library stock or its staff. However, during the project serious consideration was given to the proposition that the information officer function should be incorporated into the teaching pattern, and that an attitude of library user-independence should be encouraged among postgraduates.

SOME LESSONS LEARNED FROM THE INFORMATION OFFICER PROJECT

The information officers were concerned with all the aspects of an exploitation program except what we have called in this manual *permanent visual information,* and of course the library facilities and their organisation had to be accepted almost without change.

Perhaps the most important factors influencing the effectiveness of the work of the information officers in individual universities was, first, the sheer size of population, and, secondly, the physical distribution of library resources. For example, in ' B ', where the population was largest, the smallest number of seminars was arranged. Apart from the self-contained structure of departments with departmental libraries, the ' institutional ' problems, described in the Monteith project, appear to be present in both the old established academic institutions and the newer universities, except possibly in ' E ', where the attitude of the academic staff was influenced by experience of a well organised central library with an active exploitation program.

Library courses with a broad foundation were not generally considered useful. As with Monteith, the use of information and libraries was not considered as an educational aim in itself. The seminars and lectures were most successful when designed to fill a specific need. Almost all postgraduates were glad to receive some guidance in order to set up personal indexes, and at ' E ' some 70 postgraduates attended lectures in thesis-presentation.

There was considerable interest in machine retrieval systems at all the universities, especially during a trial period when the service was free. Retrospective searches, especially through MEDLARS, were most in demand; but after the trial period, the services were generally discontinued on the score of expense. To some extent computer selection was distrusted, especially for current information. A further factor was that research at a university is part of a training technique, so that it is not so important to save laboratory and experimental time by applying results of other people's work. The research carried out by academic staff is usually a part-time activity, where the time factor is not a particularly important consideration, so that literature searching is not carried out under external pressure. These conditions are different from those obtaining in industrial research, where there is pressure to obtain results which can be applied to commercial ends. In such circumstances, machine retrieval systems may be looked upon as good business by saving the time of highly paid staff.

Assessment of results: As with all kinds of exploitation activity, the measurement of results from the project was difficult.

The chief difficulty lies in the fact that better library exploitation stems from many causes. In a university the most important factor where students are concerned is pressure from the teaching program. The second difficulty in measurement is arranging workable sampling arrangements. In Monteith, this was made possible by very careful organisation in a very small population. In this project the information officers kept careful records of feedback information. At ' B ', questionnaires were sent out after each seminar. People who attended seminars and who returned for further advice were also recorded. The increased demand for lectures or seminars and for printed guides was further indication of a changing interest in library use. In each university, greater use of libraries and information resulted from the work of the information officers; and the example at ' E ' seems to show that an exploitation program is likely to run most smoothly where the institution is not too large, where the main resources are in a central library which is well organised, and where efforts are made to make the library easy for readers to use.

MEASURING READERS' FAILURE AT THE SHELF

This survey was carried out during two periods of eight weeks each in 1969 and 1970 in the Cambridge University Library[4] and, later, similar surveys were made at the universities of Sussex, Glasgow and Bradford, and also at a college of education in Manchester.[5] The original experiment was designed to find out:

1 What particular books were in such heavy demand that they were frequently not available on the shelves.

2 How successful readers were in finding books on the shelves which were known to be in the library (that is, were recorded in the catalogue).

3 What were the reasons for their failures.

4 What steps could be taken to reduce the chance of failure.

At Cambridge, readers were asked to record their own failure information on slips provided. These slips were hung in bundles every six feet along the library shelves. When a book was not on the shelf, the reader was asked to record on the slip, the *class mark*, the *author* and the *title* of the missing *book* or *periodical*;

also his *status* (undergraduate, BA or MA/*faculty*), and to place the completed slip on the shelf where the book should have been. MA students and faculty members could borrow books for a whole term.

During the period of the survey each book, before being re-shelved, had placed in it slips of different colours to indicate whether the book had been borrowed by MA/faculty, BA, or under-graduate, and whether it had been used in the library or had been away for rebinding. When a book which had caused a failure was reshelved, the coloured indicator slip was matched with the failure slip and placed in an appropriate collection box. To check the effectiveness of the survey, about one thousand readers were asked whether they knew that a survey was taking place, whether they failed to find the book they were looking for and, if so, whether a failure slip had been filled in. Sixty seven percent knew about the experiment and had, when appropriate, filled in a failure slip.

The information collected in this survey may be analysed in many different ways:

1 *The reasons* for failure could be ascertained.

2 *Multiple failures* could be recorded (that is, several people seeking the same missing title).

3 Subject areas where failures were most frequent would be shown up.

4 *Time* between notice of failure and the reshelving of books from different categories of borrower could be noted.

As a result of these experiments, changes in reservation and recall routines were recommended and also that books most heavily used should be borrowed for restricted periods.

In the 'failure' surveys, the function of the library is assumed to be simply to supply the needs of individual borrowers, rather than to be an active unit in a teaching program.

A STUDENTS LIBRARY RECORD AT A POLYTECHNIC
We can assume that the main purpose of a college or university is to teach or, more accurately, to provide a staff and facilities so that students will be stimulated to learn; and that the function

of the library in such an institution is to form an integral part of the teaching and learning program. Therefore, the more closely the library activity is tied into the teaching pattern, the more effective will be its role in the college or university. The readers may be considered in two groups, the students and the teachers. If these assumptions are correct, it should be possible to obtain useful pointers concerning the effectiveness of the library contribution if two kinds of information can be obtained.

1. A record of how the teaching staff plan library activity into their teaching program.

2 A record of how students use the library as part of the learning program, especially when set work by teachers which involves the use of information in some depth.

The use of a *library liaison record* to obtain information in the first area was discussed in some detail in chapter 8.

In an attempt to obtain information about the student use of the library, a supply of *student library record* forms was sent to selected lecturers at the Hatfield Polytechnic. The lecturers had previously expressed a willingness to take part in the experiment. Each lecturer was asked to hand out the *records* to the students when setting an exercise which would involve the use of information in some depth, at the same time pointing out to students that the completed *record* would form an essential part of the exercise.

Information obtained: The experiments took place between October and December 1972. About 100 completed records were returned; nine out of ten students used the catalogue; about a quarter of the number used abstracts or periodical indexes; half of them asked for help from library staff; and one in ten obtained information from outside the library.

Some lessons learnt: The sample was too uneven and too small to make general conclusions. Most of the people concerned were first year industrial engineering students who were working on projects, and who were using the library for immediate needs as part of the teaching program. The group had also received a course of library instruction. Two results were significant; first, the importance of individual assistance from library staff, and, secondly, the comparatively small use made of periodical indexes. Most of the outside information was obtained from manufacturers, but one or two had contacted research organisations.

Some pointers for the future: First, more information is needed about the kind of help library staff are giving to readers. There is probably a need for library staff generally to be more aware of exploitation techniques and this point has already been discussed (chapter 7). Secondly, these students used the *record* for the first time. If lecturers, as a general practice, demanded a record of library use and of the references found for all relevant exercises, a habit in the precise use of information could be established with students. The introduction of the use of *students library records* could usefully form part of the liaison program between the library and the academic staff when discussing the library requirements for a student project.

REFERENCES

1 P B Knapp: *An experiment in co-ordination between teaching and library staff for changing student use of university library resources. Co-operative research project no 874.* Monteith College, Wayne State University, Detroit, Michigan, USA. 1964.

2 P B Knapp: *College teaching and the college library.* American Library Association, 1959, ACRL monograph 23.

3 OSTI Project: *Information officers in universities.* To be published as Aslib *Occasional paper.*

4 John A Urquhart and J L Schofield: ' Measuring readers' failure at the shelf.' *Journal of documentation* 27 (4) Dec 1971 273-286.

5 *First failure survey at Didsbury College , Spring 1971.* To be published by Manchester City Education Dept.

Index